44 Guided Meditations For Personal Development

A Companion For Purna Asatti

Kathryn Colleen, PhD RMT

Trend Factor Press

Trend Factor Press, a division of Sparticle Concepts LLC
1530 P B Lane #M4819, Wichita Falls, TX 76302-2612
KathrynColleen.com

Copyright © 2020 by Amy Kathryn Colleen Messegee, PhD RMT. All rights reserved.

This content is protected by United States and International copyright laws. No part of this content may be reproduced or distributed without the written consent of the author.

ISBN 978-1-7348534-4-5 (paperback, English)
ISBN 978-1-7348534-5-2 (ebook, English)
ISBN 978-1-7348534-6-9 (audiobook, English)

To contact the author, or to find more information, please visit KathrynColleen.com. Your thoughts and questions are welcomed.

Cover Art by Kathryn Colleen, PhD RMT

Kathryn Colleen, PhD RMT

TABLE OF CONTENTS

Introduction

Your Personal Development Journey
10
How To Use These Mediations
12

Stage One

Grounding Yourself - Connecting To Your Time, Attention And Spaces
14
Connecting To The Emotional Roots Of Your Choices
18
Trusting Yourself
22
Trusting Your River
26

Stage Two

Connecting To Experiences
32

44 Guided Meditations For Personal Development

Connecting To Your Needs
36
Connecting To Your Body - Sleep, Regeneration And Movement
40
Manifesting - A Comprehensive And Simple Guide
45
Manifesting Struggle - Swimming Against Your River
50

Stage Three

Connecting To Your Sexuality - Mind, Body And Energy
56
Connecting To Yourself - You Are More Than Your Needs And Wants
61
Connecting To Others - Seeing Their Humanity Through Their Needs
65
Connecting To Your Internal Energy And Feelings
70
Connecting To Your Money - Getting Out Of Debt
74

Stage Four

Kathryn Colleen, PhD RMT

Connecting To Yourself - Recognizing And Removing Negative Patterns
80
Connecting To Your Ideology - Define Your Ideology And Put It Into Practice
84
Connecting To Your Money - Solidifying Your Savings Engine
89

Stage Five

Connecting To Others - Seeing Their Humanity Through Their Ideology
94

Stage Six

Connecting To Yourself - Taking Responsibility For Your Life
102
Connecting To Your Body - Setting Goals And Making Progress
106
Connecting To Yourself - Forgiving And Accepting Yourself As Human

44 Guided Meditations For Personal Development

110

Connecting To Your Heart - Breaking The Trance Of Unworthiness

115

Connecting To Others - Seeing Yourself In Others

119

Connecting To Others - Forgiving And Accepting Others As Human

123

Stage Seven

Connecting To Your Faith Through Questioning

130

Connecting To Doubt - Questioning Everything

134

Connecting To Yourself - Healing Your Scars

138

Connecting To Yourself - Identifying And Replacing Limiting Beliefs

142

Connecting To The Infinite Silence / Divine

146

Stage Eight

Kathryn Colleen, PhD RMT

Connecting To Universal Truths
152
Connecting To The Universe / Divine - Letting Go Of Knowing
156
Connecting To The Silent Observer
160
Connecting To Your Purpose - Methods For Finding It
164
Connecting To Your Reality - Designing Your Future
168
Connecting To Others - Seeing Their Truth
172

Stage Nine

Connecting To This Moment - Presence, Mindfulness And Intuition
178
Connecting Completely To Your Partner
184
Connecting To The One Consciousness
188
The Big Bang And The One Consciousness (A Thought Experiment)
193

44 Guided Meditations For Personal Development

Connecting To Your Intellect - Building Skills For Your Purpose
198

Stage Ten

Connecting To Higher Wisdom - Beyond Intuition
204
Connecting To The Oneness And Your Influence
208

Stage Eleven

Connecting To Your Reality - E=mc2
214
Seeking Complete Connection
218

Support For Your Journey

Questions, Answers And Additional Resources
224
About The Author
225

Kathryn Colleen, PhD RMT

Introduction

44 Guided Meditations For Personal Development

Your Personal Development Journey

Although it is simple, it may not be easy... This journey will not be instant. That dissatisfaction you feel is based in your soul and to feel the kind of peace that you seek, you will need to face the realities of your past choices and start consciously making better ones. You will face yourself - your beautiful reality and your dark side. Your humanity will be laid bare for you to see and you will be challenged to love yourself, not in spite of your humanity, but because of it. **On the other side of this journey, however, is a life so amazing and joyous, peaceful and content, that words will fail and all you will feel is gratitude for each day.**

If you currently enjoy a particular religion, you can use this process to develop a deeper level of faith. However, the path to get there includes questioning everything and growing to see your deity in a higher, more expanded role and from a less anthropomorphic perspective. Ultimately, you will come to recognize the immensity of your deity's reach and what they have gifted you.

Kathryn Colleen, PhD RMT

You are in good company. Although the life and path you will choose for yourself is unique, the journey is ancient and well tested. May these meditations lead you to the peace you seek.

44 Guided Meditations For Personal Development

How To Use These Mediations

These meditations support the tasks detailed in the book *Purna Asatti: A Roadmap To A Better Life Through Complete Connection*. Refer to that book for more detail on each stage and task. These meditations can be used alone, or with the roadmap for additional support.

For the greatest effect, start with Stage One and work your way forward, using the meditations to enhance and accelerate your personal development. Once you have completed them all, return to each as needed, to help maintain the beautiful stages of your choosing.

Each meditation includes guidance on what to focus on, what postures work best, how to be present, as well as a journey specific to that task and how to take the results with you into your daily life.

Audio versions of these meditations are available in multiple formats. See KathrynColleen.com for links to the audio versions of these meditations, related books, writings, podcasts and other materials to support your journey.

Kathryn Colleen, PhD RMT

Stage One

44 Guided Meditations For Personal Development

Grounding Yourself - Connecting To Your Time, Attention And Spaces

Focus

Welcome. This meditation supports the Stage One task of connecting to your time, attention and spaces. The hardest part of this task is truly internalizing that what YOU want is important, your purpose should be a priority, and you respect that. So that is where we will focus here.

Posture

Take a moment to get comfortable. You can sit or stand or lay down. It doesn't matter. You can close your eyes or keep them open. Do what works for you.

Presence

Take a slow deep breath. Let it out like a sigh of relief. Be at peace. You are here now. Take another slow deep breath, and this time, send it out slowly, consciously, with purpose, all the way. Be at peace. You are here now. Pause and repeat these breaths until you feel relaxed and at peace.

Kathryn Colleen, PhD RMT

Journey

We begin in the heart. Focus on your heartbeat. How does it feel? The physical sensation there? You are alive. You are here now. Are there emotions moving there? They grow as you focus on them. Within that movement is there love?

This is you. You are here in this life to find your gift, and to give of your gift to the world. Focus on the heart. Ask the heart. Is this true? You may feel joy welling up in your heart, or a little wave of joy that confirms: YES.

You are here, now, for this purpose. Nothing could be more important. Return focus to the heart, the heartbeat, and the emotions moving there. For in the heart is also love for others. We give of our time and energy to them. We may empty ourselves to fill them. How does that make your heart feel? The heart sinks down a bit at that idea.

Focus on the heart. The heartbeat. The emotions moving. Joy. It is so vitally important that you find your gift. It is so vitally important that you share it. Imagine taking time to find your gift. How does your heart feel?

44 Guided Meditations For Personal Development

Imagine taking time to share your gift? How does your heart feel? Full. Focus on that feeling as it grows.

NOW you have something to give. Fill your heart. Then give to others. Fill your heart. Then give to others. Your journey is of highest importance. Your gift is needed here. Can you find one hour a day for this? Ask your heart. Yes. Can you hold it sacred, as you are held sacred? You are sacred. Your gift is sacred. Ask your heart. Is this true? Yes.

Focus on the heart. For your truth is not found outside of yourself. Your truth is not found in others, their opinions or demands. Your truth is found in the heart. Listen to the beat. Urging you forward in your journey. Calling you inward to the truth.

Imagine taking the time to find your gift and holding it sacred. Imagine others respecting your time, because YOU do. Imagine finding your gift and nurturing it. How does your heart feel? Full. Joy. Love. Purpose. You are here, now.

Kathryn Colleen, PhD RMT

Return

When you are ready, bring your awareness back to your surroundings. Notice how you feel. Take this feeling with you and return to it anytime you like.

Connecting To The Emotional Roots Of Your Choices

Focus

Welcome. This meditation supports the Stage One task of connecting to the emotional roots of your choices. This is a task where you are asked to think of major choices in your life, and dig to find the true emotional roots of those choices.

The most challenging part of this task is being honest with yourself about why you chose to do what you did, without judgement. Because you need brutally honest answers here, you must not judge yourself, or regret past decisions. You must detach from your past self and view it from afar.

This meditation will support the detachment, honesty and non-judgement needed for this task.

Posture

Take a moment to get comfortable. You can sit or stand or lay down. It doesn't matter. You can close your eyes or keep them open. Do what works for you.

Kathryn Colleen, PhD RMT

Presence

Take a slow deep breath. Let it out like a sigh of relief. Be at peace. You are here now. Take another slow deep breath, and this time, send it out slowly, consciously, with purpose, all the way. Be at peace. You are here now. Pause and repeat these breaths until you feel relaxed and at peace.

Journey

We begin in the mind. Think back to a major decision in your life. Perhaps one that did not end very well. See yourself there like you are watching a movie. Feel the distance of time between now and then. See the space and time expanding between the you now and the you back then. You are not that person anymore. Time and experience have changed you. Each day, you have evolved further away from who you were, and further toward who you will be.

Bring your attention now to your heart. Feel love for who you used to be, like the love for an old friend. Mistaken, sure. We all make mistakes. But we are worthy of love.

Focus on the beat of your heart. Focus on the feelings there. Is there energy moving? Is there emotion? Let it move.

Ask yourself why that version of you made the choice that they made. Ask why again. Why, again. Keep asking why until you get to the real emotional root. Was it fear? Was it loneliness? Was it unworthiness? Was it something else? Let your heart tell you the truth.

Sit with this in acceptance for a little while. Imagine sitting with your past self, two old friends, offering compassion for the truth.

Acknowledging this truth feels freeing. Sit with this freedom for a little while. And the freedom feels like joy-love, our natural state. Yes.

The truth allows us to let this go. Feel gratitude for this truth and this release.

Return

When you are ready, bring your awareness back to your surroundings. Notice how you feel. Take this feeling with you

and return to it anytime you like. We see now how our choices multiply the emotion at the root of them. In difficult moments and major decisions, detach from your current self to acknowledge the truth. Use that understanding for better decisions.

Trusting Yourself

Focus

Welcome. This meditation supports the Stage One task of trusting yourself. Trusting yourself is a lot harder than it should be. You must come to trust your gut, or your intuition. That requires learning the difference between true intuition and impulse from the "monkey mind." This meditation will support learning how to tell the difference, so that you can act from a place of, and come to trust, pure intuition.

Posture

Take a moment to get comfortable. You can sit or lay down. It doesn't matter. For this exercise, it will help to close your eyes and focus internally.

Presence

Take a slow deep breath. Let it out like a sigh of relief. Be at peace. You are here now. Take another slow deep breath, and this time, send it out slowly, consciously, with purpose, all the way. Be at peace. You are here now. Pause and repeat these breaths until you feel relaxed and at peace.

Journey

We begin with a body scan. Start at the top of the head. What does that feel like? What sensations do you feel there? Come down a little now and focus on the front third of the brain, behind the forehead. What does that feel like? This is where the human consciousness, or the monkey mind lives. Take a moment to focus on what that feels like.

Come down further now to the heart. Feel the heart beat. Focus on what it feels like. What sensations do you feel there? What emotions stir here? Heart centered intuition lives here. Take a moment to focus on what that feels like. The truth of your soul lives here. Ask yourself, what is the truth if your soul in this moment?

Scanning further down now, to just below your stomach, near the solar plexus. If you feel fear, you feel it here. If you make decisions in fear, the result will multiply that fear. Take a moment to focus on what that feels like. We do not want to make decisions in fear. We will choose differently.

Scanning further down now to the gut. Deep in the belly, in the bowl of the pelvis. What feelings do you have there? What sensations? This space feels grounded. Expansive. This is where gut-centered intuition lives. Take a moment to focus on what that feels like.

There is no fear here. It feels wise and calm. Invite your mind to think on your choices down here, instead. There are more neurons here and around your heart, than in your brain anyway. What if we thought with our heart and gut rather than with our monkey minds? Take a moment to focus on what that idea feels like.

For a greater challenge, imagine the heart and the gut are connected by a cable that runs down your spine (because they are). What would it be to make our choices here, among the heart and gut in agreement. There is no fear here. There is love, compassion, grounding, wisdom, knowing, joy. And the results of those choices will multiply those feelings.

Return

When you are ready, bring your awareness back to your eyes, and then to your surroundings. Notice how you feel. Take this feeling with you and return to it anytime you like. As you go about your day, remember to make decisions from a place of intuition, not impulse; from a place of love, compassion, wisdom, grounding, joy and knowing, not from a place of fear, loss or unworthiness. Feel the difference in your body, and use that to improve your connection to yourself, others and your world. Practice recognizing intuition versus impulse each time you make a decision. This is a skill that will serve you daily for life.

44 Guided Meditations For Personal Development

Trusting Your River

Focus

Welcome. This meditation supports the Stage One task of trusting the river of your life, or the divine, to take you where you need to be. It can be hard to trust your river, because no life is without some measure of sadness, struggle or pain. There will be loss. There will be lessons. And we cannot see around the corner. This is true.

The key to trusting your river, or the divine, is in recognizing what you can influence and what you cannot. We must let go of what we cannot influence, and focus on what we can do, what we can change, and what we can affect.

This meditation will support understanding the difference between what we can and cannot influence and letting go of the rest. It will support peacefully and joyously flowing in your river as it takes you where you need to be.

Kathryn Colleen, PhD RMT

Posture

Take a moment to get comfortable. You can sit or stand or lay down. It doesn't matter. You will want to close your eyes for this journey.

Presence

Take a slow deep breath. Let it out like a sigh of relief. Be at peace. You are here now. Take another slow deep breath, and this time, send it out slowly, consciously, with purpose, all the way. Be at peace. You are here now. Pause and repeat these breaths until you feel relaxed and at peace.

Journey

Imagine that you are standing in the middle of a wide, calm river. The water is about waist high. The current is mild. It flows around you like it flows around the stones and rocks it encounters. You touch your hands to the surface. The water is the perfect temperature. The banks of the river are low, sloping, and covered in a lush green grass. Beautiful trees dip down to shade the sides of the river.

44 Guided Meditations For Personal Development

This is the river of your life. It has brought you to a beautiful and peaceful place. You can walk around exploring all the parts of the river, the sides, the plants, the rocks. You enjoy the sun and the shade. You feel gratitude for this peaceful place.

Slowly, the current starts to build a bit. It is becoming stronger. And perhaps the river is starting to push you forward. It is a bit more peaceful towards the sides, but so much harder to move forward there. You can move forward quickly in the middle, but the current is swift and a bit frightening. You worry that if you let go into the rapid current in the middle, you might never make it back to the peaceful shorelines. You miss the calm, peaceful place you were before. But you seem to have no choice.

But you do have a choice. You can choose to let go and flow with the now mighty current in the middle, or you can cling, unchanging and frightened to the banks. You always have a choice. What will it be?

You decide to let go into the middle. At first it is scary. The water is swift. Things are changing rapidly in the scenery all around you. But you notice, you are always above water. You can breathe just fine. You breathe deeply, knowing this breath is yours. This body is yours, this river, too, is yours. You ask the river to take you somewhere peaceful and joyous. You relax into the water's supportive and reliable cradle. It is carrying you where you need to be.

You let go. The river carries you. You trust that it will take you where you need to be. You start to enjoy the ride. Uncertainty becomes the promise of new and exciting things. The unknown makes room for big and amazing. You cannot see around the corner, but you trust, it is where you need to be. You flow with your river.

You round the corner as the river deposits you into the most beautiful, calm pool. It is peaceful. It is more peaceful than the one before. It is more beautiful than the one before. It is exactly where you need to be. You feel gratitude for the journey.

And the journey has changed you. Now you know that when the current is mild, your influence is absolute, and when the current is swift, joy is quickly found in letting go.

Can you feel the current of your river right now? Is it swift or calm? Is it time to influence and explore? Or is it time to let go and flow?

Return

When you are ready, bring your awareness back to your surroundings. Notice how you feel. Take this feeling with you and return to it anytime you like. When you are struggling against your river, use this to parse out what you can influence and what you cannot. Let go and focus on what is yours to affect, and when the time is right to affect it. Trust in your river or the divine to handle the rest.

Kathryn Colleen, PhD RMT

Stage Two

Connecting To Experiences

Focus

Welcome. This meditation supports the Stage Two task of connecting to experiences. In this task, you are challenged to let go of past experiences (good and bad), by deeply connecting with them, what they taught you, and examining how they altered your beliefs. The most challenging part of this task is actually letting go of the experience after you have analyzed it. This meditation will support releasing that experience by detaching it from your current self.

Posture

Take a moment to get comfortable. It will help to sit comfortably and close your eyes for this internal journey. As always, do what works for you.

Presence

Take a slow deep breath. Let it out like a sigh of relief. Be at peace. You are here now. Take another slow deep breath, and this time, send it out slowly, consciously, with purpose, all the way. Be at peace. You are here now. Pause and repeat these breaths until you feel relaxed and at peace.

Journey

For this journey, choose an experience that you would like to leave in the past. It could be a good experience or a bad experience. Something you would like to move beyond. Hold it lightly in your mind.

What lessons did you learn from that experience, that you can use going forward? What gifts did that experience give you? Do you love yourself more? Do you value yourself more? Are you smarter? Wiser?

View the experience as if watching a movie. You see yourself in the movie. You see other people. You see places. You see the choices made by everyone involved. When you describe the story of this experience in your head, do not say, "I." Say, "He did that. She did this. They felt these things. She made choices because... They chose to... And she learned that ..... and he learned that... and they chose differently." Keep everyone, including yourself in the third person. Tell the story to yourself now.

44 Guided Meditations For Personal Development

You feel emotion about this scene. Take a moment to connect with the emotions that you feel. It's OK to feel whatever you feel. Name it. Elation, shame, embarrassment, joy, love, hate, anger, jealously, foolishness. Just notice each emotion and name it within you. As you name it, notice where in your body you feel it.

See the emotion emerging from your body like a ball of color. Hold it with love and gratitude for what it taught you. Say, in your mind, "I have learned from this. Thank you." And release it. It floats away and dissolves into the air like dust. Take a moment to identify, locate and release all the emotions from this scene.

This experience has changed you permanently. It may not be obvious how, but it ultimately serves your good, your purpose and your future. You are not that version of you anymore. As we spin through the universe, you are literally millions of miles away from that time and place. Feel the distance between you now and those characters then. Feel the past disappearing behind you, dissolving into dust, drifting away in the wind.

Be here now. There is only here. There is only now. You are free.

Return

When you are ready, bring your awareness back to your surroundings. Notice how you feel. Take this feeling with you and return to it anytime you like. With each new experience in the future, examine what it taught you. Examine how it has changed your beliefs. Edit those beliefs to ensure they will serve you, and release that experience into the past, taking only your new self forward.

Connecting To Your Needs

Focus

Welcome. This meditation supports the Stage Two task of connecting to your needs. We have many needs: physical, mental, spiritual, medical, professional and more. In this task, you are cataloging your needs in these categories.

The challenge here is to be completely honest about what you need without judgement, and to then be willing to stand up for your needs without guilt. This meditation will support the honesty, non-judgement and strength needed for this task.

Posture

Take a moment to get comfortable. You can sit or stand or lay down. It doesn't matter. You can close your eyes or keep them open. Do what works for you. Be somewhere that you can focus intently, or somewhere that you can safely zone out of reality for a little bit.

Kathryn Colleen, PhD RMT

Presence

Take a slow deep breath. Let it out like a sigh of relief. Be at peace. You are here now. Take another slow deep breath, and this time, send it out slowly, consciously, with purpose, all the way. Be at peace. You are here now. Pause and repeat these breaths until you feel relaxed and at peace.

Journey

We begin in the mind. We are probably there already. What does you mind feel like? Is it busy? Is it calm? Is it full? Or is it lacking something? What does your mind need? You can be honest with yourself here. What intellectual or professional skills or opportunities or time do you need? Why have you not had that?

As you name your needs, you feel something. What do you feel? Guilt? Shame? Joy? Amusement? Name it. Focus on the feeling and ask why you feel this. Wait for the honest answer. Dig deep for the truth, and hold the truth in love, like you would hold a child.

Let's scan down to the heart now. What does your heart need? Why do you not have it? Explore this. Seek the truth.

Scan down now to the Lower Dantian. This is a space in the middle inside of your belly. Right in the center of the gut. When you focus on this place, you might feel it open into an infinite space. Stay with it, either way. What does your soul need?

When asking for what the soul needs, don't overthink it. Answers come quickly. Acknowledge them. Explore this for a moment.

Move outward now to your whole body. What does your human body need that it is not currently getting? What feelings come with acknowledging that?

Why are you not getting it? Are those excuses or real reasons? Dig deeper.

We have found now a list of needs, and a whole bunch of emotions that those needs bring up. And underneath those emotions is the truth of why the needs have not been met. Fear of failure, fear of success, unworthiness, laziness... It's

OK. There is not one person on this earth that has not felt these things before; and that has not been held back by these before.

Feel appreciation for these fears and doubts that have held you back. Yes, appreciation. Appreciate them for trying to keep you safe. But you don't need them anymore.

It is time to stand up for your needs. Find a way to meet them, even just a little. Choose to meet them, and a way will be found.

Return

When you are ready, bring your awareness back to your surroundings. Notice how you feel. You might feel empowered, renewed, and centered in your truth. Take this feeling with you and return to it anytime you like. Remember to attend to your needs regularly. Practice this honesty, non-judgement, and non-guilt to strengthen your ability to meet your needs as they evolve over time and through experiences.

44 Guided Meditations For Personal Development

Connecting To Your Body - Sleep, Regeneration And Movement

Focus

Welcome. This meditation supports the Stage Two task of connecting to your body through sleep, regeneration and movement. In this task, you are asked to understand how much sleep you need, and make it a priority. You are also asked to choose forms of regenerative activities like meditation, massage, hot baths, journaling or time alone. And you are asked to choose some form of movement and move your body each day.

The most challenging part of this task is making yourself enough of a priority to actually do it. It is easy to make a list of the sleep, regenerative activity and movement that you would love to have. It is quite another to make it a priority. This meditation will support the self-care mindset needed for this task to be successful.

Kathryn Colleen, PhD RMT

Posture

Take a moment to get comfortable. You can sit or stand or lay down. It doesn't matter. You can close your eyes or keep them open. Do what works for you.

Presence

Take a slow deep breath. Let it out like a sigh of relief. Be at peace. You are here now. Take another slow deep breath, and this time, send it out slowly, consciously, with purpose, all the way. Be at peace. You are here now.

Journey

We begin. Picture yourself on a typical stressful day. Notice the reaction in your body to the stress. Shoulders are squeezed up. Breaths are shallow and small. The heart is heavy and the solar plexus is hollow - empty.

Why? Focus on the heart. It is heavy because your needs for regeneration are not being met. It is heavy because it is being ignored. The heart is tired. It needs rest, and care.

44 Guided Meditations For Personal Development

Now focus on the solar plexus; above the belly button. It feels different here. It feels hollow, empty. Why? This is the center of free will and independent strength of self. Now it makes sense. You have denied the individual self. You have not spoken out for your independent needs.

This may bring feelings of shame, sadness or regret. Do not judge yourself harshly. All of these things are human. All of us have, at some point, failed to honor the independent self and its needs. We have a hundred wonderful excuses. None of which we will continue to allow.

Now choose one regenerative activity from your list. Maybe it's a hot bath, journaling, time to yourself, massage, a long walk with your love, or anything else that relaxes you and fills your soul. Take a moment to imagine doing that activity. This time is yours.

Notice how you feel now. Regenerative activities feel relaxing and somehow energizing at the same time. Now choose a second activity from your list. Take a moment to imagine doing that.

Kathryn Colleen, PhD RMT

Let's check in with the heart now. How does it feel? It feels lighter. Is there some joy there peeking through? The heaviness is lifted. Feel this.

Now we check in with the solar plexus. What do you feel there? It is not so empty anymore. Having stood up for your independent needs, you affirmed your strength of self. You feel solid... capable... even fulfilled. Stay with this feeling.

We see, from this, that self-care... regenerative activities... are about a lot more than just rejuvenating the body and mind. They are about rejuvenating the heart and soul. They affirm the independent will and strength of self. They are the source of fulfillment and joy.

And now, your soul is full. Now, you have something to give to others: joy, love, wisdom, caring, focus... THIS is why it matters. THIS is why it must be a priority.

Return

When you are ready, bring your awareness back to your surroundings. Notice how you feel. You might feel cared for, loved, and important. That is good! Because you ARE. Take this feeling with you and return to it anytime you need a boost to make your own self-care a priority.

Kathryn Colleen, PhD RMT

Manifesting - A Comprehensive And Simple Guide

Focus

Welcome. This meditation supports the Stage Two task of beginning to consciously manifest your life. In this task, you choose something that you want to change, or add to your life: people, places, things, lifestyles, experiences, and so forth. Deciding what you want is easy. The challenge here is to be honest about why you want it (because the result will multiply the root emotion), and to let go of your desire for it.

This meditation will support analyzing the root emotion behind your desire, and letting go of the desire for it, once your request is made.

Posture

Take a moment to get comfortable. It will help to sit comfortably to focus on this inner exploration. You can close your eyes or keep them open and safely zone out a bit. Do what works for you.

44 Guided Meditations For Personal Development

Presence

Take a slow deep breath. Let it out like a sigh of relief. Be at peace. You are here now. Take another slow deep breath, and this time, send it out slowly, consciously, with purpose, all the way. Be at peace. You are here now. Pause and repeat these breaths until you feel relaxed and at peace.

Journey

We begin by choosing the one thing you want to manifest the most, at this point in your life. Think on it lightly. Remain detached from it. Ask yourself... why do you want that? List the reasons to yourself in your mind.

Now dig deeper... for each reason... ask why is that so important? Why? Why? Take a little time now to honestly answer why at least five layers deep until you get to the true emotional root of the issue.

What was the root? Fear, anger, purpose, joy, love, unworthiness, failure, greed, lust? It's OK. You can certainly be honest with yourself here inside your own head. Take a moment to ensure your analysis is correct. Why do you want this?

If the root of your desire was a negative emotion, the result will multiply that negative emotion. If you feel unworthy, angry, or fearful, you would be better off to solve that first. Let go of this desire all together and ask instead to feel worthy, or to feel safe or joyous.

If the root or your desire was a positive emotion, you are clear to proceed to asking and letting go. If the root was negative, ask instead for healing.

Imagine having what you desire. Feeling satisfied, pleased. Hold your desire lightly in the back of your mind. That means, as you imagine, consciously move the thought to the back of your brain. Imagine that the thought of it is located at the back of the head. Place your awareness there and the image there, as you think of it. Take a moment to soak in having what you desire and feeling satisfied with it.

Now imagine that your desire is a coin in your hand. As you look at this coin, you can see your desire playing out on the surface like a movie. Imagine that right in front of you is a bowl of water or a pool or well. It is infinitely deep. You cannot see the bottom. When you are ready, drop the coin into the water.

If it serves your best interests, it will of course be granted. Your order was received. Let go of the desire for it. It is on its way.

Thoughts of your number one wish will pop up from time to time. When they do, imagine the coin again and drop it into the water again. Each time it comes up, acknowledge it, feel satisfied, and let it go. Practice this now a few times.

For a more advanced challenge, imagine dropping the coin into the heart, the lower dantian, or any other chakra and note the differences in how it feels.

Return

When you are ready, bring your awareness back to your surroundings. Notice how you feel. You might feel a little bit more free. You might feel a little bit more influential or empowered. Good! You have great influence. It is time to exercise it. Take this feeling with you and return to it anytime you like. We can become impatient, as the universe lines up to deliver larger requests. This too is human. Just drop the coin again and let it go.

Manifesting Struggle - Swimming Against Your River

Focus

Welcome. This meditation supports the Stage Two task of recognizing when you are struggling against your river. This task is a follow-on to the previous manifesting task. Sometimes, life feels like a struggle. In this task, you are asked to recognize that struggle, and to stop struggling.

The most challenging part of this task is recognizing struggle versus effort, and then letting go of what you thought you wanted. This meditation will support understanding effort versus struggle, and the release needed to let go.

Posture

Take a moment to get comfortable. You can sit or stand or lay down. It will help to close your eyes for this deep internal exploration.

Kathryn Colleen, PhD RMT

Presence

Take a slow deep breath. Let it out like a sigh of relief. Be at peace. You are here now. Take another slow deep breath, and this time, send it out slowly, consciously, with purpose, all the way. Be at peace. You are here now. Pause and repeat these breaths until you feel relaxed and at peace.

Journey

You have joined in this meditation because you are struggling. To begin, identify where you are struggling. What is it that you want that is just not working out. Recount it to yourself now.

Is it struggle or is it effort? Effort is just work. It is a list of tasks that need to be done. It is a skill that needs to be learned. It is time invested. Sometimes it is patience. Effort results in measurable progress. It feels good, positive, joyous, smooth and flowing. Effort towards your goal is enjoyable.

Struggle looks like misery, without any measurable progress. Struggle feels like it should not be this hard. Struggle is when others have taken the same path, in the same way, and gotten a lot farther by now. Outside experts cannot see why you should not have seen progress yet. Something is holding you back, intentionally.

That something is the universe, the divine, source, God, Allah, the Tao... whatever you want to call it. You see, the divine loves you. You are here for a reason and the divine is trying to safeguard you and your purpose so that you can carry it out. You and your purpose are being protected. Even if it is not obvious. Feel this for a moment.

If you are struggling, this path is not for you... or it is not right for you right now. If you insist, the universe may let you have it, and negative consequences may come along with hard lessons. It is time to let it go.

What if you put this path aside for just this moment? Do this now. Just for this meditation, leave this path in the past, or perhaps for another time in the future. For a moment say, "OK, we will not pursue that right now..." now you have created space for another idea to come in. A better idea, possibly.

Kathryn Colleen, PhD RMT

Focus on the heart. The center of your truth. Ask yourself, what should you do instead? Where should you place your effort now? Listen now for the answer. Be patient as it comes and do not judge it. What should you do instead? Think on this now.

What answer did you get? You may not have liked it. Or you may have felt relief. Or something between. Give the answer a try. For the next few days, or a week, take a break from the old path and try the new path instead. If the new path flows smoothly, it is for you.

Your heart knows what to do. Trust it.

Return

When you are ready, bring your awareness back to your surroundings. Notice how you feel. You might feel a bit resigned, but a little more free, and at the same time, open to new and better ideas. Take this feeling with you and return to it anytime you feel that you are struggling against your river. If the new path is also a struggle, try this exercise again to hone your ability to hear the truth of your heart. Keep trying the new path until it flows in joy.

44 Guided Meditations For Personal Development

Kathryn Colleen, PhD RMT

Stage Three

Connecting To Your Sexuality - Mind, Body And Energy

Focus

Welcome. This meditation supports the Stage Three task of connecting to your sexuality - mind, body and energy. In this task, we examine our current beliefs about our sexuality and sexuality in general, we catalog our sexual needs, and explore the energy within the body through sexuality. Your sexuality is a lot more than just your preferences. It includes your beliefs, needs, mind, body and energy. Your sexuality is a vast, varied, and rich aspect of your humanity to explore. For this meditation, we will focus on clearing the slate of old beliefs and recognizing energy within the body, from the sexual perspective.

Posture

Take a moment to get comfortable. You can sit or stand or lay down. It doesn't matter. You may want to close your eyes for this exploration. You will certainly want to be in a private place. This meditation may induce rather strong sensations.

Allow it to be whatever it is. For this journey, you will need the visual of your partner. If you do not currently have a partner, enjoy envisioning your ideal partner instead.

Presence

Take a slow deep breath. Let it out like a sigh of relief. Be at peace. You are here now. Take another slow deep breath, and this time, send it out slowly, consciously, with purpose, all the way. Be at peace. You are here now. Pause and repeat these breaths until you feel relaxed and at peace.

Journey

We have two goals here. First, let's focus on releasing old beliefs. We begin in the heart, where truth may be found. Focus on the heart. Breathe into it. When you think about the concept of sexuality, what emotions do you feel? Joy, guilt, fun, shame, something else? Do you see sexuality as inherently dirty, or pure? Sacred or base? Ask your heart ... what beliefs about sexuality are you currently holding that no longer serve you? Explore this for a moment.

44 Guided Meditations For Personal Development

Now ask your heart... what beliefs about sexuality would you like to have instead? What new beliefs could you use to replace the old beliefs? Take a moment to list these in your mind.

Now that you have some new beliefs to learn, say them over and over to yourself.

Ask your heart... can we start over now? Can we begin with a clean slate of beliefs and add just these new ones?

You are free. The slate is clean. New beliefs are in place.

With a clean slate, we are free to explore energies within the body. We will use a combination of affirmations and body-focus. From the heart, take your attention down to the solar plexus. What do you feel there? Sensations? Emotions? Name them.

As we read the following affirmations, notice how the feelings change in the solar plexus. This is energy moving. Experience this...

Kathryn Colleen, PhD RMT

You are free. You are here in this body. It is yours. You are safe in this body. It is yours. And your sexuality is yours to explore.

Place your attention now on the sacral chakra, below the navel, in the middle of the pelvis. If you are familiar with the lower dantian, it is below that.

An affirmation... This is sacred space. This is the infinite space of creation. This space is yours. You reach out from this space in connection to yourself. You reach out from this space in connection to your partner.

Place your attention now on the root chakra. This chakra is located at the perineum. Imagine energy coming down into your head, down your spine, out the root chakra and into the earth. You are a conduit for the energy.

This is the energy of connection. This is the energy of all things. This is the energy of life, and love, of your partner and of yourself.

Now reverse the direction. Pull the energy up from the earth, into the root chakra, up the spine and out the crown. Do not impede the flow. Do not keep it for yourself. All the way up and out.

What energy do you feel in the root now?

Now with each breath in, bring the energy up. And with each breath out, bring the energy down. Up. Down. Up. Down. Imagine now your partner is with you. Breathing together. As they breathe out, sending energy out of the root, you breathe in, taking that energy into the root and up, out of the crown. Then you breathe out, sending energy down and out. They take that energy in through their root chakra, and up and out the crown. Experience this for a moment.

This is oneness. This is the potential of your sexuality.

Return

When you are ready, bring your awareness back to your heart, and then back to your surroundings. Notice how you feel. Take this feeling with you and return to it anytime you like. Better yet, take this feeling and return to it with a partner.

Kathryn Colleen, PhD RMT

Connecting To Yourself - You Are More Than Your Needs And Wants

Focus

Welcome. This meditation supports the Stage Three task of connecting to yourself; recognizing that you are more than your needs and wants. In this task, you are challenged to question WHY you need what you think you need. We ask why over and over, at least five times, to dig deep into how you think this thing would make you FEEL. That is why you want it... because it would make you feel a certain way.

This task then challenges us to see that we are not our needs and wants; that we have something to offer this world. The hardest part of this task is admitting the truth behind what we believe we need. This meditation will support the brutal honesty needed for this task by tapping into the truth in the heart and in the gut as well as recognizing the emotions tied to each desire.

Posture

Take a moment to get comfortable. You may want to sit or lay down, and close your eyes for this internal exploration.

Presence

Take a slow deep breath. Let it out like a sigh of relief. Be at peace. You are here now. Take another slow deep breath, and this time, send it out slowly, consciously, with purpose, all the way. Be at peace. You are here now. Pause and repeat these breaths until you feel relaxed and at peace.

Journey

We begin. For this journey, choose something that you feel you deeply desire, or something that you would even say that you need. Hold this in your mind for a moment.

Bring your attention now from the mind to the heart. Feel the heart beating. This is a good place to explore the truth. Place the image of what you want into your heart. Imagine it literally inside your heart. Ask yourself, why do you want this?

Kathryn Colleen, PhD RMT

Take a few moments to ask why, why, why.... dig deep for the truth.

Imagine now that you have what you want. How would that make you FEEL? Be honest. What is the feeling that you seek? Freedom, worthiness, prestige, being loved, acceptance, wholeness, adventure, joy.... be deeply honest with yourself.

Now ask yourself... Why don't you have that feeling NOW? Take a moment to explore the truth of why you don't have that feeling right now, and are seeking that feeling in what you desire.

Move your attention down now to the lower dantian; to the gut... the source of infinite wisdom. Feel the expansion in that space in your body as you focus on it. Feel gratitude for the wisdom that is to come. Ask... What other ways could you find the feeling you seek, right now, in your current situation, while you await the fulfillment of your desire? Take a moment to be creative. What could you do right now?

Imagine carrying out your new idea. How would that feel? Are there new feelings there? Excitement? Joy? This is a good idea. If it feels off, go back to get another idea until it feels exciting and joyous.

Return

When you are ready, bring your awareness back to your surroundings. Notice how you feel. Take this feeling with you and return to it anytime you like. Carry out your new idea. See if that changes your desire for the original thing that you wanted. Does it refine your desire? Does it change it completely? Good ideas are all around you. Return to this source of wisdom anytime you need it.

Kathryn Colleen, PhD RMT

Connecting To Others - Seeing Their Humanity Through Their Needs

Focus

Welcome. This meditation supports the Stage Three task of connecting to others and seeing their humanity through their needs. In this task, you are challenged to put yourself in someone else's shoes, imagine their needs, and find a way to help. This is a simple enough task to do for people that you love, but it's much harder to think this way about people that you do not like at all. This meditation will support the challenge of thinking about the needs of people you don't like, so that you can see their humanity, and progress to Stage Four, as well as set a foundation for later stages.

Posture

Take a moment to get comfortable. You can sit or stand or lay down. It doesn't matter. You can close your eyes or keep them open. Do what works for you. For this exercise, we must understand that needs include a lot of things: food, clothing, shelter, love, connection, acceptance, self-worth, new skills, friendship, feeling like you are doing a good job, and more. Keep these in mind.

Presence

Take a slow deep breath. Let it out like a sigh of relief. Be at peace. You are here now. Take another slow deep breath, and this time, send it out slowly, consciously, with purpose, all the way. Be at peace. You are here now. Pause and repeat these breaths until you feel relaxed and at peace.

Journey

We begin in the head. Place your attention there. We will start with an easy one. Think of someone you care about deeply. The first person to come to mind. What is their current situation? Consider it for a moment and imagine what it is like to go through their day. What do they worry about? What is hard for them? Take a moment to walk through their day as them.

If you were them, what would you need?

Kathryn Colleen, PhD RMT

Could you provide that in some way? Maybe even just a phone call or a nice note? Or something more?

How would that make you feel to help them in that way?

Let's take this out from there now. Think of someone you know, but only a little. Maybe a work colleague that you don't see that often. Someone you are largely detached from, but are aware they might have challenges.

Move your attention, and the thought of them, down to your heart. Imagine you are them. Ask your heart... what do they need? Take a moment to imagine their needs.

You are seeing their humanity. We all have needs. We all have challenges. Send them good thoughts, in hope that their needs will be met, and their challenges made easier. Holding their image in your heart, think to yourself, "I hope your needs are met and that your challenges become easier."

When you thought those good wishes, you may have noticed energy moving in your heart. Focus on that feeling for a moment.

44 Guided Meditations For Personal Development

When you are ready, let's take on a bigger challenge for ourselves. Stay with the heart. Imagine now someone whom you do not like at all. It can be someone you know personally, or a public figure. Choose one person. Remain detached... remote... imagine a day in their life. Walk through their day and look for the challenges. What is it like to live their life? What challenges do they have?

If it was you... what would you need in that situation? What would you wish for?

You are seeing their humanity. We all have needs. We all have challenges. Send them good thoughts, in hope that their needs will be met, and their challenges made easier. Holding their image in your heart, think to yourself, "I hope your needs are met and that your challenges become easier."

Focus again on the heart. You are feeling compassion. You are seeing the humanity in others through the lens of their needs, and you are wishing good things for them.

You may also feel a little superior as you may think that compassion is beyond the person that you don't like. Back slowly away from your judgement and any notion of better-than. You have challenges too. We are all equally human. We are equally fallible. Have compassion now for yourself in learning to have compassion for others. Send love to yourself now on your own path. Smile at your own humanity coming out in this exercise.

Return

When you are ready, bring your awareness back to your surroundings. Notice how you feel. Take this feeling with you and return to it anytime you like. Practice seeing the humanity of everyone you meet by imagining their challenges and needs. And, in this way, see your own humanity as well.

44 Guided Meditations For Personal Development

Connecting To Your Internal Energy And Feelings

Focus

Welcome. This meditation supports the Stage Three task of connecting to your internal energy and feelings. In this task, you are asked to recognize and name emotions as you feel them, and seek the root cause. You are then asked to notice how emotions correlate with energy moving in your body. This helps you connect with the energy so that you can work with it later.

This meditation will support recognizing that energy, and how it relates to emotions, as well as finding the roots of those emotions.

You should note that understanding and exploring your emotions does not mean that you need to express every feeling you have out loud, or to anyone at all. This is for your own personal exploration and understanding.

Kathryn Colleen, PhD RMT

Posture

Take a moment to get comfortable. For this exploration, you will want to sit or lay down and close your eyes.

Presence

Take a slow deep breath. Let it out like a sigh of relief. Be at peace. You are here now. Take another slow deep breath, and this time, send it out slowly, consciously, with purpose, all the way. Be at peace. You are here now. Pause and repeat these breaths until you feel relaxed and at peace.

Journey

We will begin with a body scan. Place your attention inside your head. What sensations are there? Notice each breath as it fills the head. Feel the brain thinking. Take a moment to explore what you physically feel there.

What emotions are there (if any)?

All emotions are rooted in one of two things... fear or love. If you feel anger, sadness, unworthiness or another negative emotion, you are ultimately afraid of something. What are you afraid of?

If you feel joy, adventure, freedom, friendship, inspiration or another positive emotion, you are ultimately in love with something... what do you feel love for?

Let's scan down the body now. Let your attention travel down to the throat. What do you feel here? What is the root of these feelings?

Move down to the heart now, home to most of our feelings of love... What do you feel here? What is the root of these feelings?

Move down to the solar plexus now... the stomach area, home to most of our fears... What do you feel here? What is the root of these feelings?

Move down now to the lower dantian... to the gut area. You may feel an expansion as you focus on this area of the body. What do you feel here... physical sensations... emotions?

You might notice that the emotions feel different here. Was it wisdom? Grounding? A more universal kind of love? Enjoy these feelings for a moment.

Return

When you are ready, bring your awareness back to your heart... then to the head... then to the eyes.... and finally back to your surroundings. Notice how you feel.

Take all of these feelings with you and return to them anytime you like by exploring the physical and energetic sensations in your body and the emotions that go with them. When you feel an emotion, explore it to find out what you are afraid of, or what you are in love with. This will allow you to express yourself more truthfully in your relationships, and even just with yourself.

44 Guided Meditations For Personal Development

Connecting To Your Money - Getting Out Of Debt

Focus

Welcome. This meditation supports the Stage Three task of connecting to your money by getting out of debt. You have a relationship with your money, whether you want one or not. You see, money is not inherently good or bad or fearful or joyous. We attach emotions and beliefs to our money that make all the difference in whether we have more or less, and how we use it to improve our lives, and the lives of others.

The hardest part of this task is motivation. You have to be able to see yourself in a situation that you have never experienced... being debt free.

This meditation will support the joyous exercise of dream setting, giving you a vision of your future that will fuel you through this process and connect you more deeply to your money.

Kathryn Colleen, PhD RMT

Posture

Take a moment to get comfortable. You will want to sit or lay down and close your eyes for this journey.

Presence

Take a slow deep breath. Let it out like a sigh of relief. Be at peace. You are here now. Take another slow deep breath, and this time, send it out slowly, consciously, with purpose, all the way. Be at peace. You are here now. Pause and repeat these breaths until you feel relaxed and at peace.

Journey

We begin with a question.... what could you do if you didn't have to make payments on your car, on your credit cards, or on your other debts? What could you do with that money, if you didn't have to send it away?

In other words... if you could do anything, if you could live any lifestyle in any location, spending your time on anything you like... what would you do? What would you do after the long vacation and after the partying.... when things settled down and you are seeking meaningful efforts for your time... what would you do? What is your ideal life? Take some time now to dream.

Are there skills you want to have? Do you dream of paying off your home? Or traveling the world? Or just living simply? Do you dream of volunteering or teaching or getting a degree? Do you dream of being creative, or learning languages, or just playing with your kids and grandkids? Dream a little more. Live this dream in your mind.

If you were living that dream, how would you feel about your money then? Imagine checking your bank accounts as part of your dream life. You will certainly keep track of your money smartly. Imagine your monthly budget meeting with your spouse when you have no debt. You are reporting out your net worth instead... watching it go up each month. You have plenty. How do you feel about money now? Focus on this feeling for a moment.

How does this dream feel? Joyous? Exciting? It is not impossible at all. Repeat to yourself... This can be done. I am worth the effort.

Kathryn Colleen, PhD RMT

Return

When you are ready, bring your awareness back to your surroundings. Notice how you feel. Take this feeling with you and return to it anytime you like. Keep this dream in your mind as you work towards debt freedom. And remember today when you reach your ideal life. It is closer than you think.

44 Guided Meditations For Personal Development

Kathryn Colleen, PhD RMT

Stage Four

Connecting To Yourself - Recognizing And Removing Negative Patterns

Focus

Welcome. This meditation supports the Stage Four task of recognizing and removing negative patterns. This task includes recognizing the negative pattern to begin with, understanding the root cause, and making a plan to stop or replace the damaging pattern. The most challenging part of this task is digging for the root cause of why you do what you do. This meditation will support that process of digging deeper for the real cause.

Posture

Take a moment to get comfortable. You can sit or stand or lay down. It doesn't matter. You can close your eyes or keep them open. Do what works for you.

Presence

Take a slow deep breath. Let it out like a sigh of relief. Be at peace. You are here now. Take another slow deep breath, and

this time, send it out slowly, consciously, with purpose, all the way. Be at peace. You are here now. Pause and repeat these breaths until you feel relaxed and at peace.

For this journey, choose a negative pattern that you find yourself repeating. What pattern do you want to stop? Think of it for a moment. Detail to yourself how this pattern hurts you, and the fact that you want it to stop.

Journey

We begin. We are creatures of pattern. This too is human. Imagine sitting next to yourself like an old friend. Offer love and forgiveness to yourself. It's more than OK, it is only human. In this space, as your friend, you do not judge. So we can explore honestly, from a short distance. You are here now.

Think of the pattern you want to remove. Why do you do this? Take a moment to dig for the reason. How does it make you feel when this pattern happens? Sad? Lesser? Unworthy?

In repeating this pattern, you are choosing to feel that way. Why? Take a moment and seek the answer. Dig deep for the honest truth.

Why do you choose to suffer?

No one deserves to suffer. We are not here on this earth to suffer. As your friend, can you offer forgiveness to yourself? Can you imagine holding yourself in love and caring. Do this now.

Can you leave the past behind? Patterns and all? Today is a new day. Make a vow with yourself to leave the past in the past and move forward from today.

Affirm to yourself as your own guardian: I love you. You deserve to be happy. I will not let this happen again. Take a moment to sit with yourself in love and compassion. Two old friends moving forward together.

What new rules can you put in place to help break this pattern?

Kathryn Colleen, PhD RMT

Can you occupy yourself with a different pattern? A healthy pattern? A self-care pattern? What would that look like?

Return

When you are ready, bring your awareness back to your surroundings. Notice how you feel. Take this feeling with you and return to it anytime you like. It is a feeling of empowerment. You are in charge of yourself. You decide what you will spend your time doing, and what is not right for you. As you move forward, put your new rules into practice. Begin the self-care pattern that you chose and hold it sacred. We are replacing a negative habit with a positive one. Each day, hold yourself in love like an old friend to remind yourself that you deserve good things. Because you do.

Connecting To Your Ideology - Define Your Ideology And Put It Into Practice

Focus

Welcome. This meditation supports the Stage Four task of defining your ideology and putting it into practice. In this task, you begin by writing down all your beliefs; as many as you can think of. You explore where these beliefs came from and whether they are right for you now. Then, you explore the root principles behind your beliefs by asking why you believe it. The WHYs are your principles. Once you have your list of principles, you seek inconsistencies and try to make your principles consistent, noting how that may update some of your beliefs. The most challenging part of this task is digging for the principles that sit behind the beliefs. This meditation will support that exploration.

Posture

Take a moment to get comfortable. You can sit or stand or lay down. You will want to close your eyes for this internal exploration. Be in a very private place where there are no other people, so that you will feel completely open to exploring your beliefs without judgement.

Presence

For this journey, choose three beliefs that you are adamant about. You might want a list in front of you to refer to. Your most adamant beliefs might be about political issues, or social issues, or even religious issues. Choose the three issues that you feel most strongly about.

Take a slow deep breath. Let it out like a sigh of relief. Be at peace. You are here now. Take another slow deep breath, and this time, send it out slowly, consciously, with purpose, all the way. Be at peace. You are here now. Pause and repeat these breaths until you feel relaxed and at peace.

Journey

We begin. There is no judgement here; not even from yourself. There is no opposing opinion here. There is only you, and your own honest exploration. Your beliefs are your own. You can keep them, change them, or make new ones at will, anytime. This is the sovereign space of your own mind. You don't have to fit into anyone's mold here.

Consider the first of your three beliefs. State it to yourself in your mind... "I believe that...." Now let's explore. Why do you believe that? We are not exploring to change our minds. We are exploring to understand the root of this belief. Why do you believe that?

Now you have in your mind a new belief that is the basis of your original belief. Ask why again. Why do you believe THAT?

Keep asking why until you get to a statement that sounds overarching; a statement that is at the heart of it all. The true root of that belief, and probably a few others as well. You may be surprised at what the principle is. It's OK. Just let it be. It is only an exploration. See what you find.

Now that you have found an underlying principle, state it to yourself again and see where you feel it in your body. Physically, where do you light up? Now state the original belief to yourself. Where does that seem to activate in your body? This difference in physical location can help you recognize a principle versus a belief. Beliefs tend to be in the head, while principles tend to be in the heart.

Consider now the second belief from your list. Let's repeat the exploration. Ask yourself why you believe this. Ask why several times to go deeper to the root of this belief. What is the principle behind it? Take a moment to seek that.

Consider now the third belief from your list. Let's repeat the exploration. Ask yourself why you believe this. Ask why several times to go deeper to the root of this belief. What is the principle behind it? Take a moment to seek that.

You now have one, two or three principles. Could you use principles for your ideology instead of beliefs? How would that change some of your choices?

Are there inconsistencies that you should address? It's quite normal to have some inconsistencies. Just note them for now.

This was a big step forward today. Hold yourself in gratitude and appreciation for the hard exploration you just carried out. Say to yourself in your mind: thank you for this.

Return

When you are ready, bring your awareness back to your surroundings. Notice how you feel. Take this feeling with you and return to it anytime you like. When you get the chance, carry out this exploration with your other beliefs. See if you can take your list of beliefs and boil them down to just a handful of underlying principles that you can use to make choices about what is right for YOU.

Kathryn Colleen, PhD RMT

Connecting To Your Money - Solidifying Your Savings Engine

Focus

Welcome. This meditation supports the Stage Four task of solidifying your savings engine. In this task, you give your ideal life, and major motivation to keep saving, a major line item in your monthly budget. Motivation is all about having a dream that is so compelling that it drives your saving automatically.

This meditation will support the dreaming needed to create that compelling vision of your ideal life, and open the doors to the creativity needed to make it happen.

Posture

Take a moment to get comfortable. You can sit or lay down. You will want to close your eyes for this very visual exploration.

Presence

Take a slow deep breath. Let it out like a sigh of relief. Be at peace. You are here now. Take another slow deep breath, and this time, send it out slowly, consciously, with purpose, all the way. Be at peace. You are here now. Pause and repeat these breaths until you feel relaxed and at peace.

Journey

Let's begin. You may have many goals. For now, let's focus on the ultimate goal...your ideal life. Imagine that you can live anywhere, have any job, spend your day any way you like. What does a day in your ideal life look like? Don't worry about how to make it happen. We are just daydreaming. Nothing is impossible. Let's walk through it...

You wake up. What does the room look like? Are you in an apartment, or a house, or a boat?

You look out the window. Where are you? What does it look like out there?

What will your morning look like? See it in detail. See the faces of the people. See the textures and colors of what surrounds you. Hear the sounds. BE there. Take a moment to experience it.

What about your afternoon? How would you spend that?

Your evening?

What a day. You are tired now. In your room again, you feel gratitude for this amazing life. Feel that now. Feel the joy of living. You think back to when you thought this was all impossible. But here you are. Take a moment to soak it in.

Return

When you are ready, bring your awareness back to your current surroundings. Notice how you feel. Take this feeling with you and return to it anytime you like. Write down everything you saw, felt and heard. Be as detailed as you can. There is a way. When you get the chance, do the research. Find a way to make it all happen. It will certainly take a bit of money (or more than a bit). Use this vision as motivation to keep saving as much as you can. Your dream is worth it.

Visualize it - feeling it, seeing it, hearing it - often. Take the actions now that will take you there in reality. It can be done. Nothing is impossible.

Kathryn Colleen, PhD RMT

Stage Five

44 Guided Meditations For Personal Development

Connecting To Others - Seeing Their Humanity Through Their Ideology

Focus

Welcome. This meditation supports the Stage Five task of seeing the humanity of others through their ideology. In this task, you are challenged to think of someone you disagree with, and to see if you can imagine why they might think that way, given their current circumstances or their past.

The most challenging part of this task is to put aside your defensive mechanisms and simply see how their life has shaped them and their beliefs, as well as how your life has shaped you and your beliefs. This meditation will support that exploration.

Posture

Take a moment to get comfortable. You can sit or stand or lay down. It doesn't matter. You can close your eyes or keep them open. Do what works for you.

Kathryn Colleen, PhD RMT

Presence

Take a slow deep breath. Let it out like a sigh of relief. Be at peace. You are here now. Take another slow deep breath, and this time, send it out slowly, consciously, with purpose, all the way. Be at peace. You are here now. Pause and repeat these breaths until you feel relaxed and at peace.

Journey

Let's begin. Think of someone that you love... a friend or family member... who feels differently than you on some political or other issue. Feel your love for them. Imagine sending them that love and wishing that they have a good day.

Now think about their past. How did they grow up? What were the major events in their lives? What were the challenges? The traumas? The triumphs? Take a moment to imagine their past.

Now think about their current situation. How do they choose to spend their time?

Based on their past, can you see why they might choose to live the way they do now?

Based on their past and their present, can you see why they might believe what they believe? Can you see how those experiences might have led them to think that way?

If feelings of offense, anger or annoyance crop up at the thought of their beliefs, let them come. It's OK. They are only feelings. Let them come. And let them go. These feelings are an indicator that you are not entirely certain in your own beliefs. It's OK. Later you can review mediations on exploring your principles and beliefs. But for now, this is just an exploration in your mind of someone else. There is no threat here.

Did you find how their life might have shaped their beliefs?

Let's take a harder challenge. Next, consider someone you know but don't have any strong feelings about - a coworker, or acquaintance - who disagrees with you on some issue. Examine what you think you know about their past and about their current situation.

Kathryn Colleen, PhD RMT

Can you see how life experiences might have led them to think this way?

You may not know much about their past, or their present. Can you imagine a past that would have shaped their thoughts? Can you imagine a present situation that might reinforce that?

For a final challenge, consider a public figure that you do not like at all; someone who disagrees with you completely on many things. Perhaps even a leader of the opposing political party.

You may feel closed off, guarded and defensive at even the thought of them. Breathe into that feeling. Note the areas of your body where stress builds. Breathe into those areas. Imagine your breath clearing out any stress so that you can work effectively. This is about taking care of you.

You probably don't know much of anything really about their past, or how they grew up. But maybe you know a little. Imagine their past. Put yourself in their shoes. In what ways is that life challenging? How would those experiences shape your priorities? Whose love do they crave, ultimately? Whose validation did they never quite get? Are they older? Are they scared? Are they seeking to leave a legacy? What are they afraid of on a deep personal level.

It's all conjecture, but everyone is afraid of something. If you can see them as afraid, you can see them as human.

Return now to the first two people that you focused on. Can you see how they are just people, on this journey, having experiences, and trying to figure it all out?

Can you see YOURSELF, just human, on this journey, having experiences and trying to figure it all out? You are the same in this way. Just human, just trying your best. Sometimes your best is not that good. Sometimes it works. Sometimes it doesn't. There are tragedies and triumphs. There are good days and bad. There is fear and love. And there you all are. Walking the same path and somehow on very different journeys. Life changes us all.

They do not have to be wrong for you to be right. These are just opinions. These are just beliefs. And we are all just human.

You can see it now... their humanity, and your own. Take a moment to feel that truth.

Return

When you are ready, bring your awareness back to your surroundings. Notice how you feel. Take this exercise with you and return to it anytime you like. Repeat it for as many people as you can think of. Try it with people that agree with you, and those who do not.

44 Guided Meditations For Personal Development

Kathryn Colleen, PhD RMT

Stage Six

44 Guided Meditations For Personal Development

Connecting To Yourself - Taking Responsibility For Your Life

Focus

Welcome. This meditation supports the Stage Six task of taking responsibility for your life. In this task, you are challenged to look in the mirror and see the person causing 99% of all your problems. The hardest part of this task is to stop blaming others for your problems, and to take personal responsibility for solving them. This meditation will support that process of shifting from blame and pity to authority and solutions.

Posture

Take a moment to get comfortable. You can sit or stand or lay down. It doesn't matter. You can close your eyes or keep them open. Do what works for you.

If you are repeating this meditation for the second or third time, or more, consider the challenge of literally looking at yourself in the eyes in a mirror for this meditation. This form of eye gazing with the self is incredibly powerful. If this is your first time through this meditation, you may want to leave the mirror out of it for now.

Presence

Take a slow deep breath. Let it out like a sigh of relief. Be at peace. You are here now. Take another slow deep breath, and this time, send it out slowly, consciously, with purpose, all the way. Be at peace. You are here now. Pause and repeat these breaths until you feel relaxed and at peace.

Journey

Let's begin by thinking of a problem or challenging situation that you are dealing with right now. It might be an overall life situation, or some specific issue. Now detach from this situation. See it from the outside. Without judging yourself harshly, ask yourself... what choices did you make that led to this situation?

Accept where you are now so that you can work to improve the situation. This situation is your current reality. Take a moment to accept your current reality for the raw fact of its existence. This is where we are.

This is where we are, but it is not where we are going. You alone are responsible for your future. You alone have authority for your future. You alone can get you out of this situation and into a better one. It is all up to you. What will you do with that kind of authority?

Where would you really like to be? What do you want your life to look like? What do you want your life to FEEL like?

What simple thing could you do TODAY to improve your situation, even a little bit?

If you did that one thing today, how might you change your situation?

What if you did one thing to improve your situation every single day? What if you took just one little step each day? How much better could your life be in a week? In a month? In a year?

Kathryn Colleen, PhD RMT

The truth is that you are more capable than you give yourself credit for. You can make your life miserable, or you can make it amazing. You are worthy of good and amazing things. Why? Because we all are. Choose amazing. Choose to make the life you want. You have both the responsibility and the authority. Your failures are yours, but so are your successes.

Take a moment to feel the power and authority that you have to make your life good, better, and amazing. Notice where you feel this in your body. Where does it stir up emotion? Focus on this area in your body and allow the feeling of power and authority to grow.

Return

When you are ready, bring your awareness back to your surroundings. Notice how you feel. Take this feeling with you and return to it anytime you like. Now, remember that one thing you could do today to improve your situation? Do it right now, without delay. See the difference it makes and keep the momentum going. Reward yourself for your effort and action, and watch in gratitude as your life goes from challenging to good to great to amazing.

Connecting To Your Body - Setting Goals And Making Progress

Focus

Welcome. This meditation supports the Stage Six task of setting goals for your body and making progress. In this task, you choose a goal for your nutrition, another goal for your exercise and a third goal for your overall wellbeing, such as sleep or meditation. Connecting with your body by setting goals and making measurable progress builds your ability to set even bigger goals later, if you want to.

The hardest part of this task is defining the steps to your goal and just getting started. This meditation will support defining those steps and visualizing the end result for the motivation to get started.

Posture

Take a moment to get comfortable. You can sit or lay down. You will want to close your eyes for this internal visualization and contemplation.

Kathryn Colleen, PhD RMT

Presence

Take a slow deep breath. Let it out like a sigh of relief. Be at peace. You are here now. Take another slow deep breath, and this time, send it out slowly, consciously, with purpose, all the way. Be at peace. You are here now. Pause and repeat these breaths until you feel relaxed and at peace.

Journey

We begin by grounding in awareness of your body. Here you are, present in this space, in this body. Feel your hands and fingers. Move them a little. Feel your toes and feet. Feel your lungs breathe. Notice how your chest expands with each breath. You can almost feel your whole body expand as you breathe in, and soften as you breathe out.

Feel your heart beating. Feel gratitude for this amazing body. It allows you to be here in this life, enjoying everything life has to offer, carrying you wherever you want to go. It is a masterpiece of engineering. It is simple but incredibly complicated. It is practical and sacred at the same time. Take a moment to feel this.

44 Guided Meditations For Personal Development

Think now of a nutrition goal that you would like to achieve. What do you want to change about your eating habits?

What is a small change you could make today? Could you move in that direction, in small steps, and meet your goal this month?

If you met your goal, how would that feel? What would that do for you?

Now for your exercise goal... what do you want to do?

What is a small step that you could take today? Could you move in that direction, in small steps, and meet your goal this month?

If you met your goal, how would that feel? What would that do for you?

Lastly, your overall wellbeing... what goal will you choose there?

What small step could you take today? Could you move in that direction, in small steps, and meet your goal this month?

If you met your goal, how would that feel? What would that do for you?

Imagine now that you have, after just a few weeks, met all three of these goals. How does THAT feel?

What is the compound effect of all three of those goals together?

Are you ready to give this gift to your amazing physical body?

Feel love and appreciation for this body once more.

Return

When you are ready, bring your awareness back to your surroundings. Notice how you feel. Take this feeling with you and return to it anytime you like. Now go take those first steps towards your three goals right now. Keep up the momentum by taking small manageable steps each day, and by celebrating your successes.

Connecting To Yourself - Forgiving And Accepting Yourself As Human

Focus

Welcome. This meditation supports the Stage Six task of forgiving and accepting yourself as human. In this task, you reflect on past mistakes, offer understanding and forgiveness to your past self, make changes, and move on. The hardest part of this task is to let go of the past, and the regret and other emotions that may come with it. This meditation will support that release. It's time to let the past, and the past you, go.

Posture

Take a moment to get comfortable. You can sit or lay down. You will want to close your eyes for this very internal exploration.

Presence

Take a slow deep breath. Let it out like a sigh of relief. Be at peace. You are here now. Take another slow deep breath, and

this time, send it out slowly, consciously, with purpose, all the way. Be at peace. You are here now. Pause and repeat these breaths until you feel relaxed and at peace.

Journey

Let's begin. We all have some choices in our past that we wish we could change. Things we wish we could have done better, if only we knew then what we know now. Choose one of these now, for yourself, as your focus for this meditation. Take a moment to tell yourself the story.

As you recall your past mistake, feelings arise. Good. The only way to release it is to connect with it deeply. Let the feelings come. Sadness... regret... lean into them like an ocean wave. Let it come. Feel it as deeply as you are willing.

Where in your body do you feel these emotions? It is likely in the solar plexus and in the heart. Focus there and let it build.

If you find yourself focusing on specific other people who were, you believe, hurt by this, offer your apologies if you feel the need. I'm sorry.

But this was their path as much as it was yours. Each of your life journeys is playing out perfectly. You are all learning what you came here to learn. You are growing and making changes.

See your past self in this scene. Can you see how different you were then?

Can you see how, knowing only what you knew then, and surrounded by the circumstances, you made the best choice you were capable of at the time. Offer compassion for your old self. Offer love as that old self relives this event. There has been enough pain.

Can you detach yourself from your old self? Can you feel how different you are now?

What changes have you made?

Would you make the same mistake again? NO. Then the lesson is complete.

Kathryn Colleen, PhD RMT

You are not perfect. You are perfectly human. You have made mistakes. You will make other mistakes in the future. This is how you learn. But they are only mistakes.

Your mistakes will become fewer and your decisions will become better. You will trust your gut and make choices more carefully.

We are not here to live a perfectly choreographed life without error. We are here to get it wrong and then choose what is right, if only for this lifetime. Not one human on this earth is without error. Not one human on this earth is without regret. This is the human condition.

Welcome to your humanity. And you are loved not in spite of it, but because of it. The fullness of who you are would be incomplete without your mistakes and your new directions.

Imagine the scene of your mistake in front of you. It moves away from you. Farther and farther. Receding into the distance. Smaller and farther away. See a door closing on that scene as it leaves with the old situation and the old you. Say your goodbyes to it all, with love and gratitude for what you have learned.

Return

When you are ready, bring your awareness back to your surroundings. Notice how you feel. Take this feeling with you and return to it anytime you like. Knowing you are human, and prone to mistakes as you learn on this journey, make your choices carefully. Trust your gut, and be aware of your motivations. Try this meditation for any past situation that keeps coming back to you with regret, asking to be processed and released. Be grateful for your mistakes, and for your new and wiser self.

Kathryn Colleen, PhD RMT

Connecting To Your Heart - Breaking The Trance Of Unworthiness

Focus

Welcome. This meditation supports the Stage Six task of breaking the trance of unworthiness. In this task, you are challenged to see how worthy you are of your own love, and how you have had the divine light of love in you and for you this whole time. It is critical that we see ourselves as worthy of love, so that we can later see others as worthy of love.

The hardest part of this task is seeing the true self that sits inside you, rather than the self you may have developed for others. This true self helps to ignite the divine light and is very easy to love. This meditation will support acknowledging and loving the true self.

Posture

Take a moment to get comfortable. You can sit or stand or lay down. It doesn't matter. You can close your eyes or keep them open. Do what works for you.

44 Guided Meditations For Personal Development

Presence

Take a slow deep breath. Let it out like a sigh of relief. Be at peace. You are here now. Take another slow deep breath, and this time, send it out slowly, consciously, with purpose, all the way. Be at peace. You are here now. Pause and repeat these breaths until you feel relaxed and at peace.

Journey

We begin. We all encounter unworthiness at a young age. We take it with us into our adult years. But we were mistaken. We misinterpreted the actions of others to mean that we are not worthy of love. But the actions of others don't mean anything about you. Take a moment to contemplate that idea.

Your true self is loved by the divine light. Your true self is loved, and loves everyone else.

But your true self might be hiding. Afraid of the actions of others making you feel unworthy, you might have tried being what you think they wanted you to be. Let's explore...

What do you think others want you to be?

Kathryn Colleen, PhD RMT

What do those others actually want you to be?

What do you pretend to be?

What are you really like? Right down in the core of your being? The part that never changes?

That real true you made you smile. You like that version of yourself. The divine likes that version of you too. You were put on this earth to be THAT.

Focus now on your heart. Do you feel it?

The divine light of love. Love for you. Love for all. You are worthy simply because you exist... the real core of who you are, simply existing and walking this path in life... is loved by the highest love of all. And it was in your heart all this time. Take some time to focus on that feeling now and let it multiply.

You are the source of the unconditional love that you crave. And you need not be anything but who you were put on this Earth to be.

Become the parent figure that loves you unconditionally. Divine love.

You are not just worthy of it, you ARE OF IT. Take a moment with this truth.

Return

When you are ready, bring your awareness back to your surroundings. Notice how you feel. Take this feeling with you and return to it anytime you like. Offer yourself this divine love daily, and offer your true self to the world. Humanity is eagerly awaiting your contribution.

Kathryn Colleen, PhD RMT

Connecting To Others - Seeing Yourself In Others

Focus

Welcome. This meditation supports the Stage Six task of seeing yourself in others. In this task, you are asked to see their major personality traits as a reflection of some aspect of your past, present or future self.

The hardest part of this task is when someone is reflecting a warning or holding up a mirror to some aspect of yourself that you do not want to acknowledge. This meditation will support the strength to look at the truth being reflected to us by others.

Posture

Take a moment to get comfortable. You can sit or stand or lay down. It doesn't matter. You can close your eyes or keep them open. Do what works for you. If you are in a public place, you can look at the people around you for inspiration.

Presence

Take a slow deep breath. Let it out like a sigh of relief. Be at peace. You are here now. Take another slow deep breath, and this time, send it out slowly, consciously, with purpose, all the way. Be at peace. You are here now. Pause and repeat these breaths until you feel relaxed and at peace.

Journey

Let's begin. We see what we want to see in others. Sometimes we see what we need to see. Sometimes the divine is sending us a message through what we see in others. Take a moment with this truth.

Choose a person in your life. Someone you love, or like very much. What do you see as their defining personality trait, or characteristic of their life? Tell yourself the story now.

What aspect of you are they showing you? Were you like that in the past? Are you like that now? Is this an inspiration for your future? Or a warning or reminder of what not to become?

Kathryn Colleen, PhD RMT

Thank them, in your mind, for showing you this. You are fortunate to have them in your life.

Now think of someone you know only a little, like a coworker or an acquaintance. What do you see as their defining characteristic?

What aspect of your past, present or future self are they showing you?

Thank them, in your mind, for showing you this. You are fortunate to have them in your life.

Now think of someone you don't like at all. What do you see as their defining characteristic?

What aspect of your past, present or future self are they showing you?

Thank them, in your mind, for showing you this. You are fortunate to have them in your life as well.

If you are in public, look around you. Choose whomever stands out to you. Someone you don't know at all. What do you see as their defining characteristic?

What aspect of your past, present or future self are they showing you?

Thank them, in your mind, for showing you this. You are fortunate to have encountered them today.

Return

When you are ready, bring your awareness back to your surroundings. Notice how you feel. Take this feeling with you and return to it anytime you like. Consider the last person from that mediation a little more... you have never met them. So how did you come to know their defining characteristic? You put it there. You chose to see that in them, as a message to yourself. They may or may not actually be that way. But your inner self has a powerful way of shaping what you see. In seeing parts of ourselves in others, we are able to connect more easily to new people. Use this as an opportunity to connect, while understanding that you will have to dig a little to see their actual truth.

Kathryn Colleen, PhD RMT

Connecting To Others - Forgiving And Accepting Others As Human

Focus

Welcome. This meditation supports the Stage Six task of forgiving and accepting others as human. In this task, you are challenged to see that the actions of others don't mean anything about YOU. You are asked to forgive, in the sense of letting their choices be THEIRS, and seeing that they are fallible humans just like you.

This task then further challenges you to forgive and accept aspects of society, like groups of people, or societal norms, that you previously rejected. Acceptance here does not mean agreeing with or condoning. It means fully recognizing that they are a part of your current reality, and that doesn't mean anything about you.

The hardest part of this task is detaching the existence and actions of others from meaning anything about you, so that you can see their humanity and their truth clearly. This meditation will support that detachment and the forgiveness and acceptance needed to see effectively see the humanity of others.

Posture

Take a moment to get comfortable. You can sit or stand or lay down. It doesn't matter. You can close your eyes or keep them open. Do what works for you. If you are in a public place, you can use the people around you as inspiration.

Presence

Take a slow deep breath. Let it out like a sigh of relief. Be at peace. You are here now. Take another slow deep breath, and this time, send it out slowly, consciously, with purpose, all the way. Be at peace. You are here now. Pause and repeat these breaths until you feel relaxed and at peace.

Journey

Let's begin. Forgiveness is a loaded word. To forgive is NOT to condone or agree with. To forgive is to let their choices be THEIR business, not yours. Take a moment with that truth.

Kathryn Colleen, PhD RMT

Consider now someone who has wronged you in the past. They made a choice. They made a mistake. They hurt you. If you have not yet forgiven it, it is because they have not yet tried to make amends. They have not acknowledged your pain. You may feel they should be punished. Fear not, karma will have its way. We all receive what we give.

So you don't want to waste your time wishing others pain. In fact, how many hours have you wasted in thoughts of them at all? Do you really want to donate your time to them? Let's let them go quickly...

To let something go, you have to connect with it deeply. Let's acknowledge each truth in turn.

They made a choice and wronged you. Yes....

They must live with their choice. Yes...

Can you see how life has already taken its price? Would you want to be them?

Their choice does not MEAN anything about YOU. It does not IMPLY anything about YOU. YES... Sit with this truth and feel it deeply.

Thank them for the lesson. Now let them go.

Turn your attention now to some societal norm or social rule that you disagree with. Some people think it is a good rule for their lives. Yes. But you don't have to follow it. NO.

You have a choice. They don't have to be wrong for you to be right. They can follow what is right for them right now and you can follow what is right for you right now. Yes.

Lastly, consider a group of people that you have previously rejected. Acceptance does not mean agreement. You can accept that they exist. You can accept that they make their own choices for themselves. You can accept that you disagree. You can make your own choices for your own life. And it's all OK.

If you are in public, look around. If you are not, imagine a crowded place. Here we are... each on our own independent journey... crossing paths sometimes... trying to figure it out...

making the best choices for ourselves as we can at the time, knowing what we know.... not knowing what we don't know.... clueless about the future ahead... hoping for the best... sometimes encountering the worst... making better choices for ourselves on our own paths... this is what it is to be human. Here we are... each of us human... fallible... mistaken... but better each day... learning.... whole... and all in this game called being human.

Can you see it? Their humanity? Their fragile realities? Their mistakes and their triumphs? Their joy and their pain? Watch them.

See how they each try to find their way back to unconditional love. See how they look in the wrong places, until they look inside. See their journey's eventual end in their later years.... see them as old and wise, maybe grumpy or sweet. See them at the very end, seeing the truth in the light.... Just ... like ... YOU.

Return

When you are ready, bring your awareness back to your surroundings. Notice how you feel. Take this feeling with you

and return to it anytime you like. Seeing the humanity in others increases your ability to see the humanity in yourself. Enjoy this side benefit as you practice.

Kathryn Colleen, PhD RMT

Stage Seven

Connecting To Your Faith Through Questioning

Focus

Welcome. This meditation supports the Stage Seven task of connecting to your faith through questioning. In this task, you are challenged to methodically and respectfully question your faith or religion, as a means to form a deeper connection with it.

The hardest part of this task is approaching it without guilt, and with an intention of deeper connection. This meditation will support the proper intentions and mindset needed to connect through your own independent study and interpretation of your favorite sacred texts, by facilitating a conversation with the divine. It's time to speak to your deity directly.

Posture

Take a moment to get comfortable. You can sit or lay down. You will want to close your eyes for this internal journey. If you have your favorite religious texts available, you may like to hold them in your hands for this meditation, as a means to connect with them physically.

Presence

Take a slow deep breath. Let it out like a sigh of relief. Be at peace. You are here now. Take another slow deep breath, and this time, send it out slowly, consciously, with purpose, all the way. Be at peace. You are here now. Pause and repeat these breaths until you feel relaxed and at peace.

Journey

We begin. Until now, you have believed as you were taught. But lately, you see some cracks in the ideology... some inconsistencies. You wonder if what was taught is right for you...

You desire a connection with the divine. But there seems to be a divide between the divine and the human teachings about it. It is time to undertake an exploration for yourself.

Your deity has built this phase into your life on purpose to help you come closer. You are right on path. And as you read the history of your faith, and as you read the sacred texts for yourself, making your own interpretations, you do not walk alone. Take a moment to feel this truth...

Focus on your heart. What do you feel there?

Take a deep breath. Give thanks for this breath and this life. And ask the divine to be with you now. Be with me now...

You may feel energy in your heart, or behind you, or near you. You may feel the divine presence within you or around you. It is comforting and kind. It is loving and safe.

Give thanks for this connection.

Express to the divine, in your own words, your desire to explore the human history and the sacred texts and connect more deeply. Do that now...

If finding your own words was difficult, you might simply feel the intention. Or you might say: I want to better understand you. I want to study these texts. Will you guide me as I seek the interpretations that you meant for me in this life? Will you guide me?

Notice if you feel energy or emotion moving in and around you. This is your response. For it is always YES.

As you explore, there is no longer an institution between you and your god. There is only direct connection. You will be guided. You will be protected. You are so very loved.

There will be many private conversations between you and your god. THIS is the foundation for deeper connection.

Return

When you are ready, bring your awareness back to your surroundings. Notice how you feel. Take this feeling with you and return to it anytime you like. As you study the sacred texts and their history, new interpretations will stand out to you, that seem to be perfect guidance for your life right now. This is how the divine works. Enjoy this closer relationship, and all it has to offer.

44 Guided Meditations For Personal Development

Connecting To Doubt - Questioning Everything

Focus

Welcome. This meditation supports the Stage Seven task of questioning everything. In this task you are challenged to question everything from your political stances, to societal norms, your life choices, and everything else. The hardest part of this task is maintaining your sanity and some sense of grounding while everything is thrown into uncertainty. This meditation will support keeping you grounded and sane while you question everything to find what is right for you.

Posture

Take a moment to get comfortable. You can sit or stand or lay down. It doesn't matter. You can close your eyes or keep them open. Do what works for you.

Presence

Take a slow deep breath. Let it out like a sigh of relief. Be at peace. You are here now. Take another slow deep breath, and

this time, send it out slowly, consciously, with purpose, all the way. Be at peace. You are here now. Pause and repeat these breaths until you feel relaxed and at peace.

Journey

Let's begin. This is a stage of continual and rapid evolution. Each aspect of your life is being scrutinized to see what is right for you. How does your body feel? Does it feel swirling? Is it chaotic? Or stressful? This is natural. Even as we approach this stage again and again, and it becomes fun and innovative, it is naturally stressful.

Focus on your head. That swirling feeling. Yes. Lean into it. Allow it. If you want to move with it, do so. If you don't want to move, don't.

Bring your attention now down to your throat. How does that feel? This is an expressive time in your life. There may be lots of energy there. Or it may feel blocked. Is there something you are not expressing? Express it to yourself right now and see how that feels.

Bring your attention now to your heart. Feel it beating. Give thanks for this. You are here now on this journey. Thank you. What feelings are here? There is peace here. Can you sense it?

Come down now to the solar plexus, just above the belly button. It feels strong as you confidently question. It's OK to seek your own truth.

One more step down into the sacral chakra... the pelvic bowl. Things are so calm here. Stay in this place for a while.

If you can, imagine dropping down into the earth. Down.... down... down... deep into the earth. Past roots, dirt and stones.... past decades gone by... deep in the earth, there is no sound... no feeling but peace and calm... hidden away.... this is a place where you can take a break from the world above... your own private cocoon.

If it is challenging, don't worry. Just practice. Deeper each time. Let's spend a little time here in the silence, wherever you may be...

On the way back up now, when you reach your legs, imagine you are carrying earth up with you... like pulling dirt and stone right up into your legs. A little bit of your earth cocoon to take with you.

Now how does your body feel? This is grounded. Feel gratitude for this feeling.

Return

When you are ready, bring your awareness back to your surroundings. Notice how you feel. Take this feeling with you and return to it anytime you like. Whenever a day feels crazy, take a minute to ground yourself. Connect with the earth and feel its peace. Send it your crazy and allow it to absorb that for you. Try it! It will keep you sane as you question.

Connecting To Yourself - Healing Your Scars

Focus

Welcome. This meditation supports the Stage Seven task of healing your emotional scars, that is, unpacking your emotional baggage. In this task, you are challenged to recognize when your baggage has been triggered, step back from it, explore it, and release it.

The hardest part of this task is detaching from it, rather than getting caught up in it. The second hardest part is releasing it. Since these are the first and last steps in the process, this mediation will support the entire process of releasing your emotional scars so that you can move forward into your future untethered to the past.

Posture

Take a moment to get comfortable. You can sit or stand or lay down. It doesn't matter. You can close your eyes or keep them open. Do what works for you.

Kathryn Colleen, PhD RMT

Presence

For this meditation, choose an emotional scar from your past that you would like to heal. What happened in your past that has left you defensive or fearful about it happening again? What triggers you today into an argument or emotional episode? Choose just one to focus on here.

Take a slow deep breath. Let it out like a sigh of relief. Be at peace. You are here now. Take another slow deep breath, and this time, send it out slowly, consciously, with purpose, all the way. Be at peace. You are here now. Pause and repeat these breaths until you feel relaxed and at peace.

Journey

Let's begin. What triggered you recently? Tell yourself the story. What situation made you emotional... angry or sad or upset? Take a minute to detail that to yourself now.

You are having all those same feelings again. Breathe. What are you feeling?

Why?... Why?... Why?

You are afraid of repeating some past situation. What are you afraid of?

What baggage is this from your past? What happened THEN?

Is this relevant NOW? Is it really likely to happen here and now?

If the answer is NO, breathe deeply... as you exhale, thank this baggage for protecting you, but you don't need it anymore.

Breathe deeply again. As you exhale, imagine this baggage moving out of your body. What color is it? What shape is it?

Thank it again, but you don't need it anymore. Watch it with love, like you are watching a beloved pet.

Watch now as it dissolves away. Take a moment here in the silence without it.

How do you feel now?

Imagine one more time that recent situation that made you emotional. Relive it again. Does it have the same effect? Does it feel different now?

Return

When you are ready, bring your awareness back to your surroundings. Notice how you feel. If there is any emotional scar left there, repeat releasing it out of your body, holding it in gratitude and love, and letting it dissolve away. Bigger traumas may need several repetitions. Return to this process anytime you feel emotional. Recognize it. Name it. Explore it. Release it.

Connecting To Yourself - Identifying And Replacing Limiting Beliefs

Focus

Welcome. This meditation supports the Stage Seven task of identifying and replacing limiting beliefs. In this task, you detail your beliefs about yourself and about life, to sort out which beliefs are holding you back, or no longer serve you. Then, you replace them with new beliefs and retrain your brain by reading them every day for about a month.

The biggest challenge in this task is identifying those limiting beliefs to begin with, and then convincing the subconscious to reverse them. Within the meditative state, we have an opportunity to speak directly to the subconscious and speed this along. This meditation will support retraining the subconscious in your new chosen beliefs.

Posture

Take a moment to get comfortable. You can sit or lay down. You will want to close your eyes for this journey.

Kathryn Colleen, PhD RMT

Presence

For this meditation, you will need a set of two or three new beliefs that you want to "install". We choose two to three so that the mind does not tune out the repetition of a single sentence. Two is ideal, but three is possible.

Make sure these new beliefs will support your goals and not hold you back. Keep them short with as few words as possible. Take a moment now to pause and list them out.

Take a slow deep breath. Let it out like a sigh of relief. Be at peace. You are here now. Take another slow deep breath, and this time, send it out slowly, consciously, with purpose, all the way. Be at peace. You are here now. Pause and repeat these breaths until you feel relaxed and at peace.

Journey

We begin. Focus on the solar plexus. What are your goals? What do you want for your life? Think about those goals and visualize them happening.

Keep your focus on the solar plexus. Feel how the energy moves there. From here, we will release everything that would get in the way of your vision. Imagine a grey mist of all those limiting beliefs, flowing out of your solar plexus.

Speak to them in your mind. "Thank you, but I don't need you anymore." Regard them with love like you are looking at a pet or a baby animal. Breathe. Watch them dissolve away with each exhale. Repeat this process now several times...

Now there is space for new beliefs. Remember your two or three new beliefs that you want to have? Recall them now to yourself.

For each new belief, give it a shape and a color. Imagine them floating in your hands just in front of your solar plexus. As you say each one to yourself, see it move into you to become a part of the very fiber of your being. Look on them with gratitude and love.

Begin to repeat your list of two or three new beliefs over and over. Say them in your mind, ending each belief with, "YES. Thank you."

Continue this repetition over and over for some minutes right now. (Belief). Yes. Thank you. ..... (Belief). Yes. Thank you..... (Belief). Yes. Thank you.

Return

When you are ready, bring your awareness back to your surroundings. Notice how you feel. Take this process with you and return to it often. Reinforce your new beliefs every day for about a month. You will know when they are solidly part of you. Your life will change to reflect them.

Connecting To The Infinite Silence / Divine

Focus

Welcome. This meditation supports the Stage Seven task of connecting to the infinite silence or divine inside you. There is, within you, an infinite silence. You might call it the divine, or God, or Allah, or The Tao or anything else. It is the divine presence within you.

Every religion and philosophy (except maybe humanism) includes a concept that the divine is in our hearts, or that we should welcome the divine into ourselves. The reality is that it is already there. Within your finite physical being is what can only be described as an infinite space of sentient silence or divine light. This meditation will support you in connecting to that space.

Posture

Take a moment to get comfortable. You can sit or lay down. You will certainly want to close your eyes for this internal and spiritual exploration.

Kathryn Colleen, PhD RMT

Presence

Take a slow deep breath. Let it out like a sigh of relief. Be at peace. You are here now. Take another slow deep breath, and this time, send it out slowly, consciously, with purpose, all the way. Be at peace. You are here now. Pause and repeat these breaths until you feel relaxed and at peace.

Journey

We begin. Scan your body from the top down. Just explore what it feels like inside. Focus consciously on what is happening inside your body. Start at the top of your head. What does that feel like? Your ears... Your eyes...

Your neck. Maybe there are some tight muscles, or pain here and there.

Your shoulders. You can move them if it helps you to focus on them. Your arms and hands.

Your lungs, breathing... your heart beating. This is an amazing body.

Your stomach... maybe you can feel your recent meal digesting.

Keep your attention here for a while as we pause to prepare.

To really connect with the infinite silence, you must come with nothing. After all, it is hard to connect with the nothing, if you show up laden with somethings.

Imagine now, that all the worries of the day are like backpacks and bags draped around you. Take them off and put them down.

All the worries, all the roles we play, all the responsibilities and fears and expectations. Put them all down.

Put down this person living this life. Put down this human existence.

Approach the infinite silence as nothing more than your inner true self - the silent observer.

Now we take the final step. Continue scanning down through your belly. When you reach a point in your lower abdomen, notice if you find one particular spot where, when you place your attention on it with curious openness, opens into a seemingly infinite space of silence and compassion and acceptance. This spot is sometimes referred to as the lower dantian.

If you can connect with and open this infinite space within you, you can imagine sinking into it like you are sinking into a hot tub or hot spring.

Meet this infinite divine space with only your divine soul. It is such a place of peace. There are no expectations here; no attachments, no roles, no responsibilities, no identity, no physical being. Nothing but pure consciousness in the moment.

This is the perfect space to drop in a wish for anything you might want to bring into your life. Think of what you would like to happen in your life. Take the need for it, the desire or want for it, and give over that desire to the infinite divine knowing that if it is in line with your purpose, of course it will be. Drop it in.

Connecting to the infinite silence or divine is about understanding that the divine is quite literally within you and you can access it, make requests, and feel its infinite acceptance anytime you like. It is not out there in some nebulous place. The divine is right here, inside you, right now.

Take some time now to enjoy this space and this connection.

Return

When you are ready, bring your awareness back to your surroundings. Notice how you feel. Take this feeling with you and return to it anytime you like. Practice this connection often so that you can access it whenever you need it.

Kathryn Colleen, PhD RMT

Stage Eight

44 Guided Meditations For Personal Development

Connecting To Universal Truths

Focus

Welcome. This meditation supports the Stage Eight task of connecting to universal truths. Many religions and many ideologies are based on the same set of principles, or emotional roots. In this task, you are asked to explore different religions and different political ideologies to try and see what they have in common, in terms of underlying roots and principles (not in terms of specific beliefs).

The hardest part of this task is reading about what you see as an opposing ideology, without becoming defensive. This meditation will support you in detaching from your own beliefs, and exploring other beliefs in that same detached way.

Posture

Take a moment to get comfortable. You can sit or stand or lay down. It doesn't matter. You can close your eyes or keep them open. Do what works for you.

Kathryn Colleen, PhD RMT

You may want some paper near by to write down your thoughts as you go.

Presence

Take a slow deep breath. Let it out like a sigh of relief. Be at peace. You are here now. Take another slow deep breath, and this time, send it out slowly, consciously, with purpose, all the way. Be at peace. You are here now. Pause and repeat these breaths until you feel relaxed and at peace.

Journey

Let's start in your own world. Choose a political issue that you care about. It can be anything you like: immigration, guns, taxes... anything. Just pick one.

Now you are already feeling a little defensive. Where in your body do you feel this? It is probably in the solar plexus, the center of your individuality. Good. Breathe into that space. There is no danger here.

Think of your political issue. What do you think is the right thing to do there? What do you think is the right solution?

Why?... Why?... Why?.... keep asking yourself why until you get down to the principle at the heart of your belief. Take the time to explore that now...

Now that you have the principle, write it down. And ask yourself, what is the emotion at the root of this principle? Write that down too. Take a little time to just feel that emotion.

Now for a real challenge. Consider someone you know and like, who has the opposite opinion on this issue. Imagine you are them. Put yourself in their place. As them, ask yourself... What do you think is the right thing to do there? What do you think is the right solution?

Why?... Why?... Why?.... keep asking yourself why until you get down to the principle at the heart of your belief. Take the time to explore that now...

Now that you have the principle, write it down. And ask yourself, what is the emotion at the root of this principle? Write that down too. Take a little time to just feel that emotion.

Kathryn Colleen, PhD RMT

At the heart of all ideologies are principles. And each principle is based on an emotional root. These emotional roots ultimately boil down to one thing: LOVE; even if they don't look that way on the surface.

Take a moment to sit with the truth that you just discovered.

Return

When you are ready, bring your awareness back to your surroundings. Notice how you feel. Take this feeling with you and return to it anytime you like. Take the time to explore as many pairs of opposing opinions as you can. Find the truth at the heart of them all and see that it is always love.

44 Guided Meditations For Personal Development

Connecting To The Universe / Divine - Letting Go Of Knowing

Focus

Welcome. This meditation supports the Stage Seven task of letting go of knowing. In this task, you are challenged to let go of the need to know the future, and the need to know the truth about yourself and life, right now. The hardest part of this task is trusting your river or the divine to deliver the answers when you need them. This meditation will support the trust needed to let go of the desire to know.

Posture

Take a moment to get comfortable. You can sit or stand or lay down. It doesn't matter. You can close your eyes or keep them open. Do what works for you. You can look around you at this reality, or you can look inward.

Presence

Take a slow deep breath. Let it out like a sigh of relief. Be at peace. You are here now. Take another slow deep breath, and

this time, send it out slowly, consciously, with purpose, all the way. Be at peace. You are here now. Pause and repeat these breaths until you feel relaxed and at peace.

Journey

We begin. Uncertainty can be uncomfortable... disconcerting even. What will the future bring? What is right for you?

We have let go of so many things... now it is time to let go of the need to know. Or at least the need to know right now.

Consider the river of your life. See it now as a wide and beautiful river, winding through a varied environment.

Imagine yourself in the middle of this river. Maybe swimming or maybe on a boat.

The scenery is always changing. Sometimes you glide through beautiful places... strange places... scary places... amazing places... but you are always moving forward.

Somehow, your river always brings you to what you need when you need it: food, light, air, friendship, love, safety, lessons of all kinds.

And certainly knowledge. Information sits like fruit in the trees along the banks as you pass. There for the taking when you need it.

The right information at the right time, preparing you for what is next around the bend. And you do always seem to have just exactly what you need for the next phase of your journey.

Have you noticed? The river provides everything right on time.

Think now of what you would like to know. Imagine it like a small rock in your hand.

Ask the river to bring you this knowledge at the right time.

Drop your rock into the river, asking that it return as fruit to feed your journey, perfectly timed.

And so it will be.

Sit back and float along for a moment, enjoying the scenery. Give thanks to your river for this journey and everywhere it will take you.

Return

When you are ready, bring your awareness back to your surroundings. Notice how you feel. Take this feeling with you and return to it anytime you like. Visualization is a powerful method. The river here, is a metaphor for your life and for the divine. Return to this meditation anytime you feel frustrated with uncertainty.

44 Guided Meditations For Personal Development

Connecting To The Silent Observer

Focus

Welcome. This meditation supports the Stage Eight task of connecting to the Silent Observer. In this task, you are challenged to recognize your inner being and connect with this higher self. The hardest part of this task is to feel this higher self within you, because it is, well... silent. This meditation will support you in connecting to and feeling that higher self.

Posture

Take a moment to get comfortable. You can sit or stand or lay down. It doesn't matter. You can close your eyes or keep them open. Some prefer to keep their eyes open for this meditation. Try it several ways and see what works best for you.

Presence

Take a slow deep breath. Let it out like a sigh of relief. Be at peace. You are here now. Take another slow deep breath, and

this time, send it out slowly, consciously, with purpose, all the way. Be at peace. You are here now. Pause and repeat these breaths until you feel relaxed and at peace.

Journey

Let's begin. When you wake up, it's like someone else is looking through your eyes at you. This is the silent observer.

Say to yourself now, "In being, I am." Now, who said that? You might say that you said it to yourself. But your lips did not move and your vocal chords did not make a sound. But you said it. And you heard it. You said it without a voice and you heard it without needing ears.

And if you wanted to, you could imagine and relive your past or imagine your future and see it.

So there is the you that is this body and there is the you that speaks and listens and sees without needing this body at all.

This you is the combination of the mind and the silent observer. The mind thinks and expresses and imagines and feels. The silent observer observes from deep inside.

Can you feel the difference? If you quiet the mind, can you feel something present inside you? Something quiet but very present that observes and experiences this life like a video game player within an avatar?

You might call it your soul. It is tempting to call it your true being but here you are on this earth in this life, in this body with this mind and these energies and this silent observer and all of it together is what it is to be a human being.

You are a physical being, a mind-being, an energy being and a silent being, all at the same time.

Feel how you are not your body, but you are in your body and you observe your body and you operate your body.

Next, Feel how you have a mind. Watch the thoughts and feelings go by like clouds in the sky... but see that you are not your mind; you observe your mind and you operate your mind.

If you can feel your energies, see that you are not your energies, but you have energies and you observe your energies and you operate your energies.

So who are you? You are what is left. The essence of you is the silent observer that is here in this life, operating this body, this mind and these energies.

Take a moment to sit with this and feel the difference.

Return

When you are ready, bring your awareness back to your surroundings. Notice how you feel. Connecting to that true self in this way opens up a perspective that you can use to take control of your mind, body and energies and use them like an avatar, to create whatever life you want. Spend some time with this silent observer - your true self beyond this life. When you are ready, try living life AS this silent observer and see what happens then.

44 Guided Meditations For Personal Development

Connecting To Your Purpose - Methods For Finding It

Focus

Welcome. This meditation supports the Stage Eight task of finding your purpose. This is a really fun task where you seek your purpose through seven different exercises, looking for the patterns.

The hardest part of this task is just finding the time to do it, and of course, being incredibly honest with yourself. In this meditation, we will walk through three methods that are tuned to internal exploration, to help you find your purpose in this life.

Posture

Take a moment to get comfortable. You can sit or stand or lay down. It doesn't matter. You can close your eyes or keep them open. Do what works for you. You may want to have paper handy to make notes.

Kathryn Colleen, PhD RMT

Presence

Take a slow deep breath. Let it out like a sigh of relief. Be at peace. You are here now. Take another slow deep breath, and this time, send it out slowly, consciously, with purpose, all the way. Be at peace. You are here now. Pause and repeat these breaths until you feel relaxed and at peace.

Journey

Let's begin. When you were small, and you had nothing else to do, what did you choose to do?

Look back from childhood until now and ask yourself what have you always done, when nobody is looking, when you are not getting paid for it.

What MUST you do just because you cannot imagine not doing it?

What activities are just at the core of your being and always have been?

Staying with your childhood... When you were very young (3-5 years old), what did you want to be when you grew up? ... WHY did you want to be that?

Then, when you were a teenager, what did you want to be for a career? WHY?

Then, when you were in your twenties, what did you want to be for a career? WHY?

Thirties?.... keep going until you reach your present day.

Consider now all the why's. What is the pattern?

Can you combine all those why's into one purpose, mission or vocation?

Do you see connections between what you have always done and what you have always wanted to do? Take a moment to let it all come together.

Now listen to the silence intently...

Ask your question, "What is my mission?," or, "What is my purpose?"...

Kathryn Colleen, PhD RMT

Write it down exactly as you hear it or become aware of it - do not stop to interpret it. And don't dismiss it.

Now put them all together. See what you have always done... see what you have always wanted... see what the universe says... what is your purpose? Take a moment now to put it all together.

Return

When you are ready, bring your awareness back to your surroundings. Notice how you feel. Take this feeling with you and return to it anytime you like. Let me remind you that your result is not going to look exactly like anything you have seen before, so if it looks like that, you need to be more specific and carry out your mission in a more unique way, by a new method, or some other variation. Get creative and don't let anyone else's rules steer you away from your true answer.

44 Guided Meditations For Personal Development

Connecting To Your Reality - Designing Your Future

Focus

Welcome. This meditation supports the Stage Eight task of designing your future. In the last task, you found your purpose. Now that you know your purpose, it is time to design a life that makes your soul sing. This should be a fun and joyous exercise and one you will want to revisit often.

At this point, your ideology should be principle-based and therefore stable, your emotional baggage is largely unpacked and you are likely ready to focus on fulfillment and purpose rather than ego and impulse.

Posture

Take a moment to get comfortable. You can sit or stand or lay down. It doesn't matter. You can close your eyes or keep them open. Do what works for you.

Kathryn Colleen, PhD RMT

Presence

As always, be aware of the emotional roots of your choices as you make this design. Be sure to design from a place of peace, love, joy, adventure or other positive emotions so that the result will multiply those for you.

Take a slow deep breath. Let it out like a sigh of relief. Be at peace. You are here now. Take another slow deep breath, and this time, send it out slowly, consciously, with purpose, all the way. Be at peace. You are here now. Pause and repeat these breaths until you feel relaxed and at peace.

Journey

Let's begin. What does your ideal life look like? Be very very specific and brutally honest about your ideal life, even if it sounds unreasonable. Many things are easier than you think. We are just daydreaming here.

What does your daily schedule look like? Walk yourself through your ideal day.

Where in the world are you? BE there. What is the weather like?

What is "work" in your ideal life?

What does your life FEEL like?

What kind of relationships do you want?

What role does money play in your life? How do you want to feel about money?

What kind of experiences do you want to have?

Your ideal life may not look like something your family or friends would approve of. It may not look like the standard definition of success that we are all handed in school. That is OK.

Return to your vision and go deeper... what do YOU want... what does your SOUL want? Be in your truth here.

Do not design the life that you were told to want. Design the life that makes your soul sing. What do you want... the you that has always been... the you at the core of your being that was sent here with lessons to learn and gifts to offer.

Return to your vision now and go deeper... feel what it is like to live that way.

Design the life that makes your whole being burst forth with energy and makes your heart feel full to overflowing.

Return

When you are ready, bring your awareness back to your surroundings. Notice how you feel. Take this feeling with you and return to it often to make your ideal life happen. Write it all down. This is key. Then, for each element of your ideal life, research what it would take to make it happen. Don't take any one person's word on the matter. Study it from all sides on your own, and talk to as many experts as you can find. Then, start making it happen.

Connecting To Others - Seeing Their Truth

Focus

Welcome. This meditation supports the Stage Eight task of seeing the truth in others. That means seeing their intentions, their current situation, their feelings, what stage they are in, and potentially much more. No, you are not reading minds here. Humans project their intentions and state of mind openly. We cannot help sending out a signal to everyone around us, detailing our truth. You are just learning to tune in to that, connect to that channel and send something positive and helpful back.

This is particularly helpful because many people hide their pain and their challenges, suffering in silence. If you can recognize that, you can offer to help, encourage them to talk, or simply send them caring and compassion.

Posture

Take a moment to get comfortable. You can sit or stand or lay down. It doesn't matter. You can close your eyes or keep them open. Do what works for you.

Kathryn Colleen, PhD RMT

Presence

Take a slow deep breath. Let it out like a sigh of relief. Be at peace. You are here now. Take another slow deep breath, and this time, send it out slowly, consciously, with purpose, all the way. Be at peace. You are here now. Pause and repeat these breaths until you feel relaxed and at peace.

Journey

Let's begin. Choose a friend or family member. Someone you love or like very much.

Consciously connect with them. Reach out your energy towards them with the intent to connect. No expectations... just wanting to connect.

When you do, ask to be shown their truth. You are putting yourself in their shoes energetically.

You will be able to feel their current emotions, and their state of mind.

Can you see their truth now? Can you see their heart (that is, their intentions)?

Can you see their humanity? Can you see what stage they are in at the moment?

What do they need right now? Take a moment to see their full truth.

Thank them for this connection and gently pull your energy and intentions back towards yourself.

Now choose someone else. This time, choose someone that you don't particularly like or someone that you have not really connected with in the past.

Reach out to them with your energy, and with an intention to connect. No expectations. Become them. Be, energetically, in their place.

Can you see their truth now? Can you see their intentions?

Can you see their humanity? Can you see what stage they are in at the moment?

What do they need right now? Take a moment to see their full truth.

Thank them for this connection and gently pull your energy and intentions back towards yourself.

Imagine your energies moving now down and into the earth with every exhale. We need to ground ourselves here before we finish. Imagine all that was these other people, is flowing down into the earth. The earth absorbs it all and will transform it, returning it to them.

Now pull energy up from the earth into yourself. Imagine it flowing up your legs with every inhale. It feels solid... green and brown... safe and protected.

Return

When you are ready, bring your awareness back to your surroundings. Notice how you feel.

Try the same technique as you pass strangers on the street. You do not need to stare at them, just a glance and the intent to reach out and connect with your energy is enough. If they catch your eye, smile and send them peace, joy or whatever you feel they need... all as you pass by.

Just because you can see people's truth and intentions now does not mean that everyone you meet will be kind. There will always be people in earlier stages who cannot see your humanity yet and may do you harm. But if you can see the truth of their intentions and their hearts, you can protect yourself. By connecting with others in this way, you can better understand them, better protect yourself, and better help those in need, all at the same time.

Kathryn Colleen, PhD RMT

Stage Nine

44 Guided Meditations For Personal Development

Connecting To This Moment - Presence, Mindfulness And Intuition

Focus

Welcome. This meditation supports the Stage Nine task of connecting to this moment through presence, mindfulness and intuition. In this task, you are challenged to explore the truth of a crowd, connect to what you cannot see, and connect even more deeply to intuition and the truth of the moment itself.

If worry is about the future and regret is about the past, then being here in the present moment is one way to significantly reduce the worry and regret in your life. That is a great start. But this moment has so much more to show you. This is a challenging exercise in all respects. This meditation will support the entire process start to finish.

Posture

You will need to be in a public place for this meditation. A coffee shop, restaurant or park works nicely. Sit somewhere

where you can see people and things, but do not need to interact with anyone. Keep your eyes open.

Presence

Take a slow deep breath. Let it out like a sigh of relief. Be at peace. You are here now. Take another slow deep breath, and this time, send it out slowly, consciously, with purpose, all the way. Be at peace. You are here now. Pause and repeat these breaths until you feel relaxed and at peace.

Journey

Let's begin by being mindful of your surroundings.

That is, pay attention and observe your surroundings in a detached but focused way. What does that mean? You have already connected to the Silent Observer. Watch your surroundings as that Silent Observer.

Just be here in this moment now, taking in the sights, sounds and feelings around you.

Notice people, colors, textures, smells, and every detail.

44 Guided Meditations For Personal Development

If your mind wanders towards thinking about tomorrow or last week, gently bring it back.

This is an active mindfulness. If you are not used to it, it can feel a little intense. Stay with it.

When you feel connected to this moment across all your physical senses, reach out with an intent to connect with the people here in this moment. This is just like connecting with other people individually, but this time with a group. Project your energy out from yourself, towards each person around you, painting the group with your energy and presence in a general way as you glance around the space.

If this is challenging, try connecting with each individual quickly until you have connected with the group. Our intent in this exercise is not to explore each person's truth, but the truth of the crowd and this space in this moment.

You are now connected to everything you can see.

Now here is the challenging part.... connect with what you cannot see. Imagine connecting with the energy and presence in the air. Imagine that the air itself is full of the energy of everyone here, of everything here, and of the place itself. Like static energy before a storm, it fills the air. You cannot see it, but you can feel it.

This is the energy of the moment; pervasive and touching this moment all over the world and beyond. Feel how your energy connects to it, and is part of it.

Questions about the past or future are not going to be answered here, but anything you could want to know about the state of things right now or the best choice to make right now is yours. Remain detached from it - that is, be the Silent Observer, connected to this moment.

In this moment, is infinite information about the present state of people, places and things. Anything you could want to know about what is happening right now, you can know: how someone is feeling, their intention, whether you are safe or not, the right thing to do, or what not to do.

Now ask your question. What do you want to Know?

Let answers come to you. This is your intuition.

44 Guided Meditations For Personal Development

For a more advanced challenge, when deeply connected to this moment, feeling the collective energy of everything and everyone in the space, can you feel how the people are all the same; just people, going through life, trying to figure it out, making mistakes, living in stages, all ultimately on the same journey?

Can you see how the things in this space are all the same... just physical objects all made up of the same basic atoms?

Now, can you feel the sameness of the people, things, and this space itself... all made up of the same atoms and energies but taking various forms like pixels in a video game? They all look different but are all ultimately just bits of energy. Spend some time with this now.

Return

When you are ready, bring your awareness back to your surroundings. Notice how you feel. Practice it to make your intuition stronger. When you drive or walk down the street, stay connected to each moment. Read people, places and things in this way, and let your intuition guide you. The more you trust it, the stronger it gets. Your intuition can guide you

Kathryn Colleen, PhD RMT

on small things, like finding a great restaurant, and on big things like crafting your ideal life. When you are in this moment, fully connected, flowing with your river, your intuition is a constant guide.

… *44 Guided Meditations For Personal Development*

Connecting Completely To Your Partner

Focus

Welcome. This meditation supports the Stage Nine task of connecting to your partner. This is a vast and years long task with many different facets. In this task, you are challenged to connect with your partner in terms of trust, safety, grounding, sexuality, strength of self, compassion, love, expression, intuition, wisdom and divine nature. That's a lot!

This meditation will support that process by helping you to focus on what you love about your partner, to see their divine nature, and to express that to them to deepen connection. You can use this meditation at any step of your couple's work to boost your connection and motivation.

Posture

Take a moment to get comfortable. You can sit or stand or lay down. It doesn't matter. You can close your eyes or keep them open. You can hold a picture of your beloved or close your eyes and imagine them. Do what works for you.

Kathryn Colleen, PhD RMT

Presence

Take a slow deep breath. Let it out like a sigh of relief. Be at peace. You are here now. Take another slow deep breath, and this time, send it out slowly, consciously, with purpose, all the way. Be at peace. You are here now. Pause and repeat these breaths until you feel relaxed and at peace.

Journey

We begin the day you met. Go there now. Relive this moment. How did you feel? The excitement and potential of new love. Was it magic? Was it funny? Feel thanks for that experience.

In these early days… What was it that drew you together? What was it that put you in awe of them? What was it that gave you joy? What about them made you thankful?

Time has passed… return to the present. You have both evolved from the experience, and from the course of your lives. What now puts you in awe of them? Feel awe and amazement for them. What now gives you joy in their presence? Feel joy for them. What about them are you thankful for? Feel gratitude for them.

Imagine now a future together. Deeply connected. Trusting. Grounded. Safe. Exciting. Each of you secure in your own independent selves, walking your journeys together, reveling in each other's purpose, in constant expression of love, joy, amazement, and gratitude. Deeply and completely connected. And so it will be.

Reach out to your partner with your energy and intention. Can you see how they glow? They are the divine light itself here on this earth and you get to be a part of that. You are the divine light itself here on this earth, experiencing your own divine nature, observing your love's divine nature. Shiva and Shakti. The divine split in two to experience reuniting again.

Look at your love. What do you see? Say it to yourself. Now say it to them.

Feel now the fullness of your heart... Your crown... your whole being lit up with love, joy, awe, gratitude. Yes. Bring this to your love and be with them.

Kathryn Colleen, PhD RMT

Return

When you are ready, bring your awareness back to your surroundings. Notice how you feel. Take this feeling with you and return to it anytime you like. Express yourself to your partner often. Let them feel your love as joy, awe and gratitude. Allow that expression to deepen your connection.

44 Guided Meditations For Personal Development

Connecting To The One Consciousness

Focus

Welcome. This meditation supports the Stage Nine task of connecting to the One Consciousness. In this task, you are challenged to experience the realization of the idea that there is only one consciousness, and you are an extension of that.

Posture

Take a moment to get comfortable. You can sit or stand or lay down. It doesn't matter. You can close your eyes or keep them open. Do what works for you.

Presence

Take a slow deep breath. Let it out like a sigh of relief. Be at peace. You are here now. Take another slow deep breath, and this time, send it out slowly, consciously, with purpose, all the way. Be at peace. You are here now. Pause and repeat these breaths until you feel relaxed and at peace.

Kathryn Colleen, PhD RMT

Journey

We begin by connecting to this moment, as we have done before...

Be mindful of your surroundings. Observe your surroundings in a detached but focused way. Watch your surroundings as that Silent Observer.

Just be here in this moment now, taking in the sights, sounds and feelings around you.

Notice people, colors, textures, smells, and every detail.

If your mind wanders, gently bring it back.

This is an active mindfulness. Stay with it.

When you feel connected to this moment across all your physical senses, reach out with an intent to connect with the people here in this moment, painting the group with your energy and presence in a general way as you glance around the space.

You are now connected to everything you can see.

Now, as before, connect with what you cannot see. Imagine connecting with the energy and presence in the air.

This is the energy of the moment; pervasive and touching this moment all over the world and beyond. Feel how your energy connects to it, and is part of it.

As you practice connecting to each moment, connecting within that moment to your intuition, and starting to feel the sameness in all things, reach out within that connection, and feel what it is like to BE these other people. Put yourself energetically in their place. What does it feel like to be them in this moment?

It is a subtle feeling. It is not intense. But if you focus, and practice, you can feel within your gut, what it feels like to be them. Does it feel confident? Insecure? Joyful? Playful?

Then, have an open mind here. This exercise has an important point... feel what it is like to BE that table, or that chair or that plant. Does it feel stable, heavy, low, tall, fragile, cold, warm, metallic? Can you feel the qualities of the wood or plastic or leaves without touching it?

Kathryn Colleen, PhD RMT

Spend a little time looking around the room and FEEL what it is like to BE other people, places and things.

You may be surprised to find you can feel it. You can feel what it is like to be anyone, or anything. Previously you could IMAGINE what it was like to be them, or at least what you would feel like if that were you, but this is different... you can actually put your energy in their place and FEEL their truth in this moment.

It is time to question... how can you do that? How is it that you can place your consciousness into theirs? How can you step into their consciousness with yours?

Because it is the same consciousness.

Think about the oceans and rivers of the world. They are all connected. Rivers flow into oceans, which flow into other oceans, and connect to other rivers. It is all one big body of water.

But, the river looks and acts very different from the sea. Why? Local environments influence how they look, how fast they flow, what fish live there, how they are used and more.

It is the same with people. We are all one big consciousness, but our local environments (as a child and today) influence how we look, how we act, and what we do in this world. We are extensions of the same single consciousness, each influenced by our local environments, but one all the same, like the river and the sea, infinitely connected.

Contemplate this. As you are deeply connected to this moment, ask your intuition if this is true. Ask if you are ready to allow this. This is a big step. Take your time.

Return

When you are ready, bring your awareness back to your surroundings. Notice how you feel. Welcome to Stage Ten. Take this feeling with you and return to it anytime you like. This is a rather advanced meditation. Regular practice will be well worth it.

Kathryn Colleen, PhD RMT

The Big Bang And The One Consciousness (A Thought Experiment)

Focus

Welcome. This meditation supports the Stage Nine thought experiment called The Big Bang And The One Consciousness. This is a fun thought experiment with some profound ideas. We present it here in the form of contemplative meditation.

Posture

Take a moment to get comfortable. You can sit or stand or lay down. It doesn't matter. You can close your eyes or keep them open. Do what works for you.

Presence

Take a slow deep breath. Let it out like a sigh of relief. Be at peace. You are here now. Take another slow deep breath, and this time, send it out slowly, consciously, with purpose, all the way. Be at peace. You are here now. Pause and repeat these breaths until you feel relaxed and at peace.

Journey

We begin with tiny things.... imagine yourself in a physics lab... experiments have shown that both photons (massless) and electrons (massed) behave like waves until measured / observed and only then collapse into a particle, and that this physical existence as a particle is temporary, lasting only as long as observed. This "observation" is defined as, and has been shown to be, the concept being generated in the mind of a sentient human being.

The intent to see a wave gives us a wave. The intent to see a particle, results in a particle.

Yet other experiments on electrons in energy wells show that all matter is energy, existing everywhere all the time (according to a probability density function) until our observation collapses its wave function, forcing it to "choose" a location in which to exist in physical form.

Therefore, sentient consciousness creates everything. Nothing exists until a sentient consciousness conceives of it.

Kathryn Colleen, PhD RMT

Everything exists as energy, until a sentient consciousness manifests it (collapses the wave functions) into what we call matter.

So here is the really interesting question: how and when did the FIRST sentient consciousness come into existence?

The first sentient consciousness could not have come into physical existence without first existing as energy. Let's approach this logically.

Either:

(1) There was a time post-Big-Bang when NO sentient consciousness existed, or

(2) A sentient consciousness always existed since the Big Bang (and possibly before).

Let's start with the first case. Suppose that there was a time, after the big bang, when this universe had no sentient consciousness (in energy form or otherwise). During this time, no wave forms would collapse from observation and thus everything would exist as energy everywhere all the time and physical objects would not come into existence. It would be a universe of 100% energy only, with no consciousness.

There would be nothing to manifest the manifestor or create the creator, and a sentient consciousness itself would never come into existence, much less planets, stars, and people.

Therefore, it cannot be true that, at the big bang there was not a sentient consciousness but that later there was. Thus, a sentient consciousness always existed, at least since the Big Bang, and maybe before.

What if the big bang was the BIRTH of a sentient consciousness?

What if, in the field of potential existence, consciousnesses springs into being - each a universe birthed by a big bang. This consciousness is consumed in creative play in a space of energy within itself, creating more and more complicated things: particles, forces, stars, planets, plants, creatures...

Every religion in the world has a deity. This deity existed, they say, since the beginning and created everything. But what was there to create with? There was only the deity. Everything was therefore made from that deity, by that deity.

This is the one consciousness. And so as we trace existence all the way back, we see that we (people, places, stars, etc.) are all extensions of the one consciousness, made by the one consciousness, from the material of the one consciousness.

This original sentient consciousness is within us - we are all part of the same whole that manifested us and we can also in turn manifest new things. We humans are part of the larger consciousness. We are physical manifestations of the original consciousness, and we are embedded with that consciousness, and as such can, and desire to, create and play and manifest. We are everything, everywhere, through all time. If there is a universal creator - we are part of it, and it is in us and around us... we are the part and whole of it.

Return

When you are ready, bring your awareness back to your surroundings. Notice how you feel. Return to this meditation anytime you like for a little fun melding physics, consciousness and religion.

Connecting To Your Intellect - Building Skills For Your Purpose

Focus

Welcome. This meditation supports the Stage Nine task of building skills for your purpose. In previous exercises, you found your purpose. Now, you are challenged to think through what skills you will need to carry it out. If your purpose is something you have never really done before, it may not be obvious, and may be a scary idea. This meditation will support seeing the possibilities of new skills that support your purpose.

Posture

Take a moment to get comfortable. You can sit or lay down. You will want to close your eyes for this internal exploration and visualization.

Presence

Take a slow deep breath. Let it out like a sigh of relief. Be at peace. You are here now. Take another slow deep breath, and

this time, send it out slowly, consciously, with purpose, all the way. Be at peace. You are here now. Pause and repeat these breaths until you feel relaxed and at peace.

Journey

We begin with purpose. What are you here on this earth to do? What are you here to learn about? What are you here to give? What is your gift to humanity? Imagine yourself living that purpose.

What skills and knowledge will you need to make the best possible effort towards your purpose?

Do you need to learn specific software tools and apps?

Do you need another language?

Do you need physical skills or abilities?

Do you simply need more knowledge about certain subjects?

Even if these skills sound impossible, consider them anyway. Many things are easier than you think. And you are definitely smarter than you think.

For extra inspiration, what skills and knowledge have you always wanted to try, do or experience? It is no coincidence that these things are related to your purpose.

As you think about these skills and knowledge, there will be, guaranteed, a voice inside your head that tells you this is crazy, or you aren't smart enough or it will never work, etc. We all have this negative voice that works to pull us towards mediocrity. Any effort to forward yourself will be met with this negative voice. And the greater the effort, the louder the negative voice. Good. It is a sign that you are on the right track.

Choose one of these skills to focus on. Imagine that you have that skill, or that certification, or that knowledge. Imagine what you would do with that.

How do you feel? Is there joy? Is there gratitude? Feel these deeply as you visualize your life of purpose.

Take a few minutes now to soak in this feeling and in this scene.

Return

When you are ready, bring your awareness back to your surroundings. Notice how you feel. Take this feeling with you and return to it anytime you like. Now, make a plan to get those skills and that knowledge. For large or intimidating skills and learning, break it down into small parts that you can do each day. If you are learning a language, start with one word per day. If you need to read a big stack of books, start with one page or one chapter per day. Learning a new app or software tool? Start with one tutorial video per day. Starting with small efforts gives you momentum and progress that will build naturally. You will quickly have the skills and knowledge you need.

44 Guided Meditations For Personal Development

Kathryn Colleen, PhD RMT

Stage Ten

44 Guided Meditations For Personal Development

Connecting To Higher Wisdom - Beyond Intuition

Focus

Welcome. This meditation supports the Stage Ten task of connecting to higher wisdom, beyond intuition. In this task, you are invited to connect with divine guidance. In Stage Nine, you practiced connecting with your intuition by connecting deeply with each moment. Now that you recognize that there is only one consciousness, and you are an extension or part of that, you have access to a higher level of wisdom and guidance.

In moments when you need, or simply would like divine guidance, it is yours. This meditation will support you in connecting to that guidance.

Posture

Take a moment to get comfortable. You can sit or lay down. You will want to close your eyes for this connection.

Kathryn Colleen, PhD RMT

Presence

Take a slow deep breath. Let it out like a sigh of relief. Be at peace. You are here now. Take another slow deep breath, and this time, send it out slowly, consciously, with purpose, all the way. Be at peace. You are here now. Pause and repeat these breaths until you feel relaxed and at peace.

Journey

We begin. Listen intently to the sounds around you... Listen now intently to the silence between the sounds. Be still and listen. Ask for guidance... May I be guided.

Feel your presence as the one consciousness.

Feel the divine nature of that consciousness.

Reach out through this infinite existence.

Feel the presence of other extensions of that consciousness here to guide you.

Have you ever felt, intuitively, the presence of a long lost family member? Or a dear friend who has left this physical existence? Do they appear to you in dreams? You can feel their presence now, if you want to. Ask for them.

With practice you may be able to see them, audibly hear them, or feel physical contact from them. If that is not the case, or you do not want that kind of experience, you are not any less connected.

They are here to help, regardless. They are conduits of divine wisdom and guidance to help you carry out your purpose.

If you can learn to hear their guidance speaking through your intuition, you can accelerate towards your purpose and your ideal life.

What would you like to have guidance on? Ask for that guidance now...

If answers came, don't dismiss them. If answers did not come yet, ask that they be made clear and obvious for you.

If the idea of guides assigned to you feels humbling, that is a good thing. We are too often taught that we do not matter. We too often feel that we would not be missed. But the divine has a purpose for you and has sent help to make it happen. If that makes you feel important, it should, because you are. You are the only one who can carry out your unique purpose.

Your purpose may be simple or grandiose, but the effect of reaching even one person with true connection can change the course of humanity. And the whole of creation is looking forward to it.

Return

When you are ready, bring your awareness back to your surroundings. Notice how you feel. Take this feeling with you and return to it anytime you like. Your guides will make you feel compelled to do what is in your highest interests. Pursue what you are compelled to do but carefully note why you are compelled (do not pursue activities driven from a place of ego, fear, or other negative emotions). As you learn to distinguish compelling from impulse, recognizing higher wisdom becomes easy.

44 Guided Meditations For Personal Development

Connecting To The Oneness And Your Influence

Focus

Welcome. This meditation supports the Stage Ten task of connecting to the oneness and your influence. In this task, you are challenged to practice experiencing existing as the physical, or as the energy, and alternating back and forth between. This is fun and difficult at the same time. This meditation will support the entire effort.

Posture

You might choose a public place or start with a private one. Take a moment to get comfortable. You can sit or stand or lay down. It doesn't matter. You can close your eyes or keep them open. Do what works for you. For some, keeping the eyes open is actually easier and more effective.

Presence

Take a slow deep breath. Let it out like a sigh of relief. Be at peace. You are here now. Take another slow deep breath, and

this time, send it out slowly, consciously, with purpose, all the way. Be at peace. You are here now. Pause and repeat these breaths until you feel relaxed and at peace.

Journey

Let's begin. At this point, you recognize both your physical body and the one consciousness that is within your body and within all people, places and things.

Feel what it is like to be your body. Sense your head… your neck and shoulders…. your chest, heart, lungs… your belly and organs… your legs, arms, hands, feet…. a total body. Situate your awareness as only this whole body.

Now feel the energy inside you. Reach out with that energy, expanding outward.

Expand your awareness into this space, connecting with the energy in this space in this moment. The energy in the air is like static electricity. Be that energy.

Connect with the things in this room. Be one object or another. Be one person or another. Just the physical side.

Switch back to the energy. You are not physical at all. You are only the energy inside and around everything.

Back to the physical. Grounded in your body. Grounded in some other object. Feel what it is like to be that object.

Back to the energy. Be the energy in that object... the energy in the room... the energy in yourself....

The energy as a pervasive encompassing whole everywhere.

The physical as all the physical matter in the room at the same time.

Take a moment to alternate back and forth... matter and energy.

You will find that you can fairly easily control how you choose to exist in this moment. You are always WITHIN this physical form, but you can be the energy or the physical.

Return

When you are ready, bring your awareness back to your surroundings. Notice how you feel. Take this feeling with you

and return to it anytime you like. This meditation can be like a workout. It can be somewhat intense and exhausting. Practice helps it become easier. Have fun with it and try it often in different spaces, public and private.

44 Guided Meditations For Personal Development

Kathryn Colleen, PhD RMT

Stage Eleven

44 Guided Meditations For Personal Development

Connecting To Your Reality - E=mc²

Focus

Welcome. This meditation supports the Stage Eleven task of connecting to your reality, where energy and matter become one. In this task, you are invited to the realization that there is no difference between matter and energy. This is a major step. This meditation will support that realization and help the human mind make sense of it with a little Physics.

Posture

Take a moment to get comfortable. You can sit or stand or lay down. It doesn't matter. You can close your eyes or keep them open. Do what works for you.

Presence

Take a slow deep breath. Let it out like a sigh of relief. Be at peace. You are here now. Take another slow deep breath, and this time, send it out slowly, consciously, with purpose, all the way. Be at peace. You are here now. Pause and repeat these breaths until you feel relaxed and at peace.

Kathryn Colleen, PhD RMT

Einstein was right. Energy IS matter. Literally. There is no difference. It is a fact of Physics that most of us ignore, even the Physicists. You have some experience now connecting to moments as the energy or as the physical form. It is time to dissolve any separation between them.

Journey

Let's begin... be here in this moment, as you have before. Connect to the energy in this space.

Connect to the physical objects in this space.

Connect to the people.

Now connect to the energy again.

This time, as you focus on existing as the energy, look at some object in the room.

Think about how sparse these physical objects are. Each atom is far far more than 99.9% empty space.

And what is in that space? Nothing but the energy binding it all together, not any physical matter.

So that table or chair you are looking at is far less than one percent solid. Can you feel the energy go right through that object?

Can you see it almost start to dissolve in front of you as you focus on its energy instead of its physical existence?

Look at the room around you now. Can you focus on the energy and see it?

When doing this exercise effectively, you will see a kind of hazy blur within the room.

With practice, you might even witness the dissolution of objects and people.

But for most of us, it is a feeling that things are about to break apart and dissolve into the energy.

It can be a little intimidating and you might find yourself holding back intentionally as the human mind fears losing itself. Nothing bad will happen if you relax into this and allow the energy to dissolve the physical.

Take a few minutes to try it. Allow this dissolution as you observe it. This is not doing or forcing, but allowing it to be.

Return

When you are ready, bring your awareness back to your surroundings. Notice how you feel. This is a similar experience to psychedelic compounds, but we have arrived here without that. If you find you could use some help reaching this state, psychedelic compounds will certainly do the trick but are not necessary. Methods such as "Wim Hof breathing" and focused mediation will give you an equivalent boost. This state of mind is an altered consciousness and very hard to maintain even for the most practiced person. Take this feeling with you and return to it anytime you like.

44 Guided Meditations For Personal Development

Seeking Complete Connection

Focus

Welcome. This meditation supports the Stage Eleven task of seeking complete connection. This is the ultimate goal. In this task, we are challenged to continue our growth with the goal of remaining as connected to every part of our lives as possible: experiences, needs, money, others, ideologies, self, purpose, energy, consciousness and the immutable oneness of it all.

That is a lot to keep track of. This meditation will support seeking complete connection by stepping us through the stages to check for any new or leftover issues that need to be addressed. It is a sort of house cleaning and self care for your soul.

Posture

Take a moment to get comfortable. Sit with your eyes closed for this active, yet internal confirmation.

Kathryn Colleen, PhD RMT

Presence

Take a slow deep breath. Let it out like a sigh of relief. Be at peace. You are here now. Take another slow deep breath, and this time, send it out slowly, consciously, with purpose, all the way. Be at peace. You are here now. Pause and repeat these breaths until you feel relaxed and at peace.

Journey

We begin. Ground yourself in your body, centered in the lower dantian. Take a moment to center there by scanning down from the head.... down to the heart... the solar plexus... and the lower dantian. Allow the expansion that happens here... an opening.

Feel love and gratitude for this existence. Feel the body and the energy as one.

1. We are open to all

2. What new experiences did you have? What did you learn? ... Give thanks for these experiences and let them go.

Thank you. They too are in the past. A new you moves forward.

3. What do you need now? ... how will you provide that for yourself? ... Thank you.

4. What others are in your attention? What do they need? ... Can you help? See yourself doing what you reasonably can. Then let it go. Their path is their own.... Thank you.

5. What new beliefs do you have? .... are these helpful or limiting? Give thanks for the helpful beliefs and let the limiting ones go.... Thank you.

6. We are all here on our own paths, walking separate journeys together. Each unto themselves... Thank you.

7. What popular belief is in your attention right now? Do you think this is right for you? How would you adjust that for your own path?... Take a moment to question this and make changes as needed... Thank you.

8. What is your purpose? Why are you here? ... What actions will you take towards your purpose today? ... Thank you for this life and this purpose.

9. Feel yourself as consciousness, and as body... Thank you.

10. Feel yourself existing as the One Consciousness, and the body... Thank you.

11. Feel yourself existing as the One Consciousness and the physical manifestation simultaneously... and there is no difference. Matter in energy. Energy in matter. All the same... all you... one... Thank You.

Return

When you are ready, bring your awareness back to your surroundings. Notice how you feel. Take this feeling with you and return to it anytime you like. As you craft a routine that helps to keep you in later stages, include activities that deepen your connections: exercise, mediation or prayer time, time to think, time to connect with your partner, and whatever else works best for you.

44 Guided Meditations For Personal Development

Remember that you still have needs, you still have an ideology (based on principles at this point) and you still have a self (all necessary to get through the day) - attend to them, evolve them, but do not ignore them and do not become attached to them.

Remember that life will take you around the circle many times but YOU are in control of how much time you spend in each stage. Recognize when you are cycling through the stages again. Take care of any new or leftover tasks from those earlier stages and bring yourself back to the later stages as efficiently as possible.

Here is to your amazing life and your complete connection.

Purna Asatti.

Kathryn Colleen, PhD RMT

Support For Your Journey

44 Guided Meditations For Personal Development

Questions, Answers And Additional Resources

Do you have questions about what you have read here? Go to KathrynColleen.com and send in your questions. Kathryn will answer you back as quickly as possible and may include your question on the podcast or blog.

Also at KathrynColleen.com, you will find:

- Links to the full edition of the book, *Purna Asatti*, which includes specific exercises for personal development plus art and poetry for a different perspective on each stage.

- The music album, *Purna Asatti - Music For Complete Connection*, that accompanies the book.

- The podcast, *On Life And Being Human*, where many of your questions may be answered.

- Other books, albums, essays and art by Kathryn Colleen.

- And more!

Kathryn Colleen, PhD RMT

About The Author

Dr. Amy "Kathryn Colleen" Messegee, PhD RMT is an American-born author, composer and artist better known for her foundational work: *Purna Asatti*, a process and practice that uses connection to self, others and every aspect of your life for managing challenges and accelerating self development.

Her summer job at 16 was doing scientific research at NASA. Before her 25th birthday she earned her Ph.D in Mathematics and was speaking to conferences on human reasoning and how to make the infinite finite. A hyper-polymath, her career has enjoyed a ride through...

- academia (as a professor of Mathematics),

- defense technology (as a Scientist, CTO, and DARPA Program Manager),

- online media (as founder of a business website and video podcast with a reach of 1.3 million),

- venture capital (advising VC firms on evaluating technologies and reading the founders for their true intent),

- private education (as founder of a local network of elite tutors and private instructors),

- and her current passion: global peace, human connection and energy work.

In each of these, the theme is always the same: aggregating seemingly unrelated perspectives to distill a new approach for accelerated results. She has published many books, hundreds of articles and papers, dozens of unique art pieces and released multiple music albums.

She is known for taking only four students each year but influences and leads thousands around the world in more than 70 countries through speaking, writing, music, art and podcasts.

She is a Reiki Master Practitioner/Teacher and is travel-proficient in nine languages which she is learning simultaneously while living out her dream of traveling the

Kathryn Colleen, PhD RMT

world, speaking at pop up events and aggregating insight on life, the universe and being human.

See KathrynColleen.com for more information, books, articles, music, podcasts, and resources.

44 Guided Meditations For Personal Development

www.ingramcontent.com/pod-product-compliance
Lightning Source LLC
Chambersburg PA
CBHW070533090426
42735CB00013B/2963